MUSCLE AND HEART

Fort McMurray Fire Stories

Design Editor & Publisher Dee Bentley

Content Editor Cyndy Pickersgill

©2017 Dee Bentley, Alisa Caswell, Trish Collins, Katherine Giesbrecht, Jonathan Gillies, Michael Hill, JD Hunter, Christina MacKay, Elizabeth Matte, David Oger, Cyndy Pickersgill, Wina Reid, Diane Schuldt-Zundel, Joe Wenisch, Danelle Wilson, Thomas Zimmermann.

1. Fort McMurray Wildfire 2016, 2. Canadian History, 3. Inspirational

4. Authors

All rights reserved. No portion of this book may be reproduced, stored in a retrieval system, or transmitted in any form or by any means—electronic, mechanical, photocopy, recording, scanning, or other—except for brief quotations in critical reviews or articles, without prior written permission from the publisher:, Dee Bentley Books: http://www.deebentley.com

ISBN-13: 978-1542303019

ISBN-10: 154230301X

This book is dedicated

to all the

Emergency Responders

of the

Fort McMurray

Wildfire

2016

Thank You

Co-Authors

Meet the contributors and follow their accounts through the phases of the wildfire.

Dee Bentley (poet) feels buffaloed by unexpected love for Canada's north. She has been published in Fort McMurray media and elsewhere for two decades, including articles, columns, short stories, poetry, cartoons, and to be released picture books.

Alisa Caswell (engineer) has lived in Fort McMurray for 16 years. She currently lives in Timberlea with her husband, two children, one dog, and a bunny.

Trish Collins (storyteller) has called Fort McMurray home for the past 16 years. The daughter of a Newfoundlander with a colourful past, and a Vancouver Island native with a penchant for embellishing reality, she has grown up in a world of telling tales and finding amusement in situations both ordinary and beyond belief. She has been applying her passion for storytelling to her teaching practice at Keyano College since 2005.

Katherine Giesbrecht (quilter) moved to Fort McMurray in 1996 where she met, married and continues to live with her husband. In 2005 they adopted their cat Moped from the local SPCA.

Jonathan Gillies (firefighter novelist) moved to Fort McMurray as a child and has called the beautiful northern community home for most of his life. As an adult, he served in the Canadian Forces with the Infantry, deploying twice to Afghanistan. He has since returned home, married and currently works for the Fort McMurray Fire Department in service to the community he loves.

Michael Hill (layperson) was born in Fort McMurray in 1981. After spending five years in the Canadian Armed Forces, he returned home in 2006 and began a career as a Heavy Equipment Operator. He is currently working on an online ministry, www.HeHasAnswers.com which he hopes will help many people know God in the coming years.

JD Hunter (radio announcer & reporter) works as a Music Director, Announcer & Community Advocate with KAOS 91.1 in Fort McMurray since September 2014. During the Horse River Wildfires of 2016, he was able to speak with over 30 radio, television and news agencies throughout Canada including Global News, Maclean's, The Globe & Mail and CTV News. He's thankful for God's comfort, grace and the opportunity to broadcast hope throughout the Regional Municipality of Wood Buffalo at this key time in history. He'd love to hear from you: Jeremy@KAOS911.com.

Christina MacKay (public relations) is a proud mother to three little boys aged 5 years-old, 3 years-old, and 3 months-old; and wife to her firefighter husband. Presently her days are filled with diaper changes, feeding, and school and activity drop-offs. But in between maternity leaves she has held various positions in public relations and marketing, and spends any free time she can manage delving into her passion for writing. She plans to write a novel and children's stories.

Elizabeth Matte (artist) has lived in Fort McMurray since 1980 and finds her work with children as a Respite and Developmental Aide rewarding. She enjoys spending time with her grown sons and grandchildren, extended family and friends, as well as painting. This is her first attempt at writing.

David Oger (firefighter with three sons) was born and raised in Surrey, BC. He moved to Alberta in 1998 and has resided in Fort McMurray since he joined the Fort McMurray Fire Department in 2003. Dave met his wife Jennifer in Fort McMurray and now enjoys family life with her and their three sons. They attend NorthLife Church, and are involved in ministry there.

Leaving northern Ontario, **Cyndy Pickersgill** (composer) moved to Fort McMurray in 2007 and gratefully called it home until October of 2016 when she and her husband Al took up residence in Spruce Grove. She loves to write fiction and non-fiction, poetry and music. She composed a song to commemorate those who gave so much during the fire, (https://www.youtube.com/watch?v=4T7SNtKy6aU). Almost an empty-nester, she is learning life without her eight children close by and finding God is teaching her contentment in every situation.

Wina Reid (backcountry enthusiast) lived in Fort McMurray for almost 35 years, and has moved since the fire. She is a wife, mother of four and grandmother of three. She held positions at Macleod's, Telstar Video, Keyano College, and the RMBW. She is currently retired and loving life; living with her husband and pup in the country.

Diane Schuldt-Zundel (active living devotee) has lived in Fort McMurray for 12 years. She lives in Beacon Hill with her husband, two children and one fish named Susan.

Roger Smith, (camper). His name was changed, however the events retold are true.

Joseph (Joe) Wenisch (RCMP & Harley rider) is a staff sergeant with the Royal Canadian Mounted Police. He was transferred to Fort McMurray in 2006 where he met his wife, Deborah, who was born and raised in Fort McMurray. Deborah joined the RCMP in 2011 and they both transferred to Lloydminster in 2014. Both responded to the call of duty to Fort McMurray at the beginning of the wildfires. They have a blended family of five adult children and one granddaughter.

Danelle Wilson (work-at-home mom) lives in Fort McMurray with her husband, Drew. She spends her days as a full time mom, raising their two children. She often looks for new ways to be creative and enjoys walking outside with the kids.

Mary Wood (pseudonym).

Thomas Zimmermann (father to seven children) is a very busy man, (or not busy enough, depending on perspective!). With seven children and a lovely wife, he finds time in the wee hours to pursue his passion of writing. Thomas has written articles for various magazines, including music and band reviews, automotive related stories, and personal anecdotes regarding the busyness of life with a large family.

PART I
BEFORE

ALBERTA

Dee (poet)

Fort McMurray is a remote city 435 km north-east of Edmonton, Alberta. Its neighbourhoods are islands in a sea of trees; mostly crown land with mining leases, SAG-D (steam assisted gravity drainage) plants, and forestry operations.

From a float plane in the air, one is blinded by reflecting sunshine from a plethora of lakes, ponds, rivers, and streams, snaking north and dumping into Lake Athabasca at the southern border of Wood Buffalo National Park.

Administrative staff up north work straight days, but mining employees are usually on rotating shifts. Some stay in camps, leaving the area for days off; but the ones who settle with their families become a close-knit community: tight circles of friends sharing child-care and carpooling to kids' activities; the city vibrant with seasonal celebrations and events.

To me, Fort McMurray was a dusty, wind-blown speck of nothing when I first arrived in 1980 from what I thought of as the centre of the universe: Southern Ontario. The population was somewhere around 29,000. I'd come to visit my father who worked at one of the oil sands mines, and stayed. I hated it for the first few months until I made friends. At that time, oil companies provided rent-control and a buy-back policy on houses for their employees.

There was a beer strike that summer so the locals only had watery American thirst-quenchers and they hurried to stock up before the Abasand access road was cut off by a wildfire playing havoc on the greenbelt. Homeowners hosed down their yards and fences, roofs, and alleyways before firefighters arrived. Problem averted; it was back to business and life..

I attended Fort McMurray Composite High School, (the only secondary school at the time), later Keyano College, gaining employment at an oil sands plant office and mine where I worked for five years. During that time, I met an all-Canadian west-coast guy; Jeff. Our dream was to leave the northern isolation and move to Vancouver Island to fish for salmon and grow food.

Before you could blink we were married and had three children to raise. It was a busy, fun, challenging time, and we narrowed our focus while life sped up. The town of Fort McMurray grew up around us, becoming a city and then amalgamating with neighbouring communities — Anzac, Gregoire Lake Estates, Janvier, Conklin, and the town of Athabasca to the south; Fort McKay, Fort Fitzgerald (population 8), and Fort Chipewyan to the north — to become the Regional Municipality of Wood Buffalo.

We took long walks in the woods and learned plant names. We camped by lakes and fished the rivers for Walleye.

FORT MCMURRAY

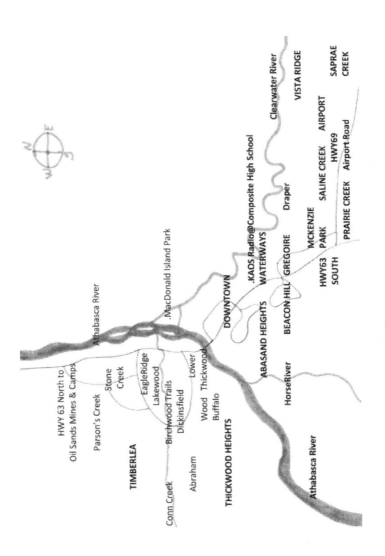

We grew vegetables and perennials. On trips to the Rockies, we traced the Athabasca River back to the mighty Athabasca Falls just outside Jasper, and to its origin at the Columbia Ice Fields. The Clearwater River flows from Saskatchewan and earned a Heritage River designation. Trappers' cabins (and a few year-round homes) dot the shoreline, reminders of the Northwest and Hudson's Bay Companies who were the first white settlers, intermarrying with the Indigenous people.

The fur trade spurred on the development of Waterways, which later became a neighbourhood of Fort McMurray, but in the early 1900s, while oil sands mining was in the experimental phase, the local industry was salt mining, which took place between Saline Creek and the Hangingstone River. The mine operated until the 1950s. The present day river valley neighbourhoods are: Downtown, Grayling Terrace, Waterways, and Draper. Additionally, the Horse River runs in a valley west of Beacon Hill and Abasand Heights, and flows into the Athabasca River.

Summers are hot and dry with dramatic thunderstorms which end as quickly as they began. The forest explodes in wildflowers and thick brush. It was common to have a few smoky days from forest fires close or far. At times the highway south would close for a few hours or a few days.

When our kids were older, I took a job with Tourism and led groups through an oil sands operation. Some days the smoke was so thick we couldn't see the mine from the Steepbank

Viewpoint. On those days, we sealed up our homes, closing windows and turning on fans to keep cool. Stuck inside, we looked forward to trips out of town.

Many Fort McMurray families evacuate in the summer; at least for a few weeks to visit relatives. Families routinely make the sacrifice to live in the north to keep their families together. The sacrifice often provides for one work-at-home parent. Dads on paternity leave may be rare, but they do exist in Fort McMurray.

A surprising number of tourists venture to Fort McMurray to see oil sands mining. They drive Highway 63 north following the divided highway to the first two mines: Suncor, which began as The Great Canadian Oil Sands Company in the 1960s; and in the early 70s, Syncrude. When you drive past, you see some activity, but mostly you see trees. And sometimes, when they aren't hiding, you may see a small herd of wood bison, reintroduced as part of extensive reclamation.

The neighbourhoods constructed during the early years of Fort McMurray are: Beacon Hill, Gregoire, Abasand Heights, Thickwood Heights, and the beginnings of Timberlea. An acreage subdivision sprang up near the airport, Saprae Creek, along with a downhill ski facility, Vista Ridge. Paths were cut in between Thickwood Heights and Timberlea creating the Birchwood Trails with groomed cross-country ski trails in the winter, walking and biking trails in the summer.

Neighbourhoods developed in recent years: Wood Buffalo, Lakewood, Eagle Ridge and Parson's Creek in Timberlea; a new section of Abasand Heights; Prairie Creek and Saline Creek on Airport Road. Abraham is the newest, slated to house seniors, a health centre, and three additional places of worship for growing congregations.

The population swelled to over 100,000 a handful of years ago, and the camps could house many thousands more. The latest downturn in the economy saw an exodus of temporary workers. It was viewed as time to take a breath and make headway on infrastructure.

There are now five high schools fed by public and separate schools in every neighbourhood, as well as two charter schools. The average age hovers around 30, and about 100 babies are born each month at the hospital.

We eventually came to think of Fort McMurray as the best kept secret in Canada with its income potential, comfortable housing, interesting friends, outdoor and indoor recreation, and no long lines anywhere (except at Tim Hortons). Sure, we took to shopping online quite a bit, and the drive to Edmonton was the precursor to any trip; and in the winter it would get so cold our tires had a flat spot so we jostled down the road until we hit black ice and did a three-sixty.

OIL SANDS MINING OPERATIONS/CAMPS

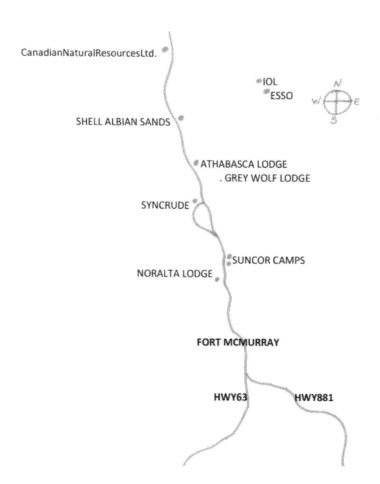

But most of us had four-by-fours, and we plugged in our block heaters, so there were no snow days. We'd chuckle at other centres warning students and employees to stay home with their freshly fallen inch of white. Often we drove in it for five or six months. We were winter professionals.

The cycle of boom and bust has rolled through Fort McMurray regularly. My husband and I bought our first house just before a drop in the economy in the 80s. It was a decade before our house could have sold for our buying price, but we held on. The next wave of boom meant many of our friends left. Home values multiplied and they decided to make a life elsewhere while they were ahead. New friends moved in, and we carried on.

People who live in Fort McMurray are accustomed to saying goodbye. And we are good at making new friends and making others feel welcome. We cheer development, happy to see a new recreation complex, more shopping, choice in eateries. But our favourite cafe is still Mitchell's for the best turkey and cranberry sandwich in the world, on signature Sunshine Bread.

What makes some locals angry are transient workers, people not invested in the community, tossing trash from their truck windows, shedding stacks of bitumen-dirt wherever they park, flipping cigarette butts out of their windows, letting white plastic single-use bags fly and dot the beautiful northern boreal.

When Mayor Blake decided to clean up the city by implementing a bag-ban, we switched to reusable bags for grocery shopping, and the city provided recycling containers and began a pilot project to produce local products from waste. Not bad. People in the North do care about the environment and are even proud of improved technology to reduce carbon emissions.

Those who really settle in, who truly enjoy the north, are the ones who skate, ski, toboggan, hunt, fish, get on the water with a boat of any sort, and generally stop fighting the elements and work with them.

Warmer climes are not immune to problems with nature. They may have tornadoes, hurricanes, earthquakes, floods (we had a few of those, too), mudslides, et al. We seemed safe in our wooded wonderland. We talked about moving south in the future, but where? We thrived in the expansive twenty-hour summer days, and cocooned in the midnight days of winter. We had our own community of friends and coworkers. We had everything we needed.

PART II
THE START

Roger (camper)

April 23, 2016

Roger Smith woke in the night from disturbing nightmares. Images of Armageddon flashed through his mind. But where? In his city of Edmonton? It couldn't be... but it looked like a Canadian city. Or was it? Perhaps it was somewhere in the Middle East. Some horrible disaster with explosions and terrified people: fire, smoke, mothers with babies fleeing.

An inaudible voice told him to pray for the people. He shook his head and tried to ignore it, but he couldn't. Roger finally slipped from his warm bed onto the bedroom carpet, leaning into his mattress with his elbows.

"Lord, I don't know where or when, but whatever disaster is coming, don't let anyone die in the flames. Please protect them all, and bring them all out. Amen."

Later that week at a prayer meeting, Roger told his friends about his dream. The group members each prayed for the terrified people in the coming disaster.

Jonathan (firefighter novelist)

I work with the Fort McMurray Fire Department as an Emergency Medical Technician and Firefighter. That sunny morning in May I was assigned to the ambulance, which meant I focused my mind on the city's medical calls despite the flurry of recent wildfires in our region.

The number of fires was no surprise – it was an uncharacteristically hot and dry springtime, after a mild winter. There had been two fires within city limits that our department and Forestry had put out days prior. But there had also been a third fire.

This one was originally further away than the two in town and was outside of our jurisdiction. It was being fought by provincial firefighters; but as it steadily approached the town, tensions increased.

On May 2nd, the fire suddenly seemed to stop and looked to be blowing away from us; it was predicted that it would avoid Fort McMurray altogether.

Thomas (father to seven children)

I wasn't sure if the wood smoke I smelled was coming from my clothes or still lingered in the air, but I couldn't escape it. We had just returned to our house in Gregoire after a voluntary evacuation the night before because of the wildfire west of us.

I had taken my lovely wife to the airport the day before so she could embark on a much needed rest, joining her mom on a quilting cruise to Alaska. (I know, I had no idea they had those, either.) I would take care of the kids with the help of a family friend while I continued to work my shift, my lovely would have an exciting adventure, and life would be good, right? I had no idea what was about to happen. Then again, no one did.

It was Monday morning, and because of the late night voluntary evacuation the previous evening, I kept the group of seven with me. Little Princess Olivia (my blonde haired, blue eyed four-year-old) helped me make pancakes, we played games, everyone went to the park down the street or rode bikes in our little circle. Life was almost normal, except Mom wasn't there.

The skies were clear Monday morning; crystal blue actually. But, as I was to find out later that was only due to what's called a temperature inversion, causing the smoke from wildfires to lay low; a false sense of security and safety.

After the outside temperature warmed, about two in the afternoon, smoke started to billow in huge clouds to the west of our little house, and grey ash fell from the sky like dirty little snowflakes, coating Vincent the Van, the camping trailer that was still hooked to him and probably everything else in Fort McMurray.

It was almost pretty, save for the angry smoke in the sky attempting to block out the darkening red sun.

 On Monday evening, I assured my seven babies that everything would be all right. Daddy would make sure nothing harmed or hurt them, and that we would evacuate again together if need be. Kisses and hugs, bedtime stories read, eyes shut and sleeping kids. Daddy went outside and looked at the sky as night fell. All I could see were many dangerous shades of red from the west. And lots of thick, black, angry looking smoke. The radio said everything was under control, but to be ready just in case. I slept fitfully that night, waking to listen to the radio, checking social media, looking outside--anything to somehow find reassurance that my little group of seven would be okay.

Alisa (engineer)

On Sunday, May 1st, we were sitting on the back patio. My daughter and her friends were selling lemonade out front. It was hot and they were making lots of money. Suddenly, my daughter burst through the back door.

"Mommy, Mommy, something exploded!" she yelled. She pointed to the white cloud of smoke on the south east side of the city.

We shrugged it off. "They'll get it", we assured her, pointing to the water bombers overhead. Later that evening, I slipped out to the Esso to fill the van.

JD (radio announcer & reporter)

Sunday May 1st was the final day of the Trade Show. I was there until about 5:30 pm. Once I left MacDonald Island Park and the Suncor Community Leisure Centre, walking through the parking lot, I noticed the first big plume of smoke coming to my right.

And when I saw that, I had a feeling inside that said that this was a big deal and it wasn't just one of the typical plumes of smoke, or even like anything else we've seen in the city over the past years.

So I left MacDonald Island Park with some anxiety in my chest, knowing this was probably going to be trouble as it was close to town.

Monday came around and things started to get a little crazier. It was raining ash. My stomach was churning all around, knowing things were escalating. As Monday went on, I didn't eat anything during the day. I took my lunch time (from work at KAOS Radio Downtown in the Composite High School) and just drove around.

Later that evening, a good friend came to see me from (one of) the sites. He convinced me to eat, so we went and got a burger from Dairy Queen. I was really thankful later that I'd eaten, because the next time I'd eat wouldn't be until 4 pm on Wednesday.

I went to bed that Monday night (in Timberlea), thinking I should have gotten an emergency kit together, but then planned to go home the next day during my lunch and do it then.

Tuesday May 3rd was a beautiful morning, not even a cloud in the sky, sun shining. When I looked at it, I thought everything was going to be okay.

Trish (storyteller)

Sunday, May 1st

I made French toast and bacon, washed the car, and took a nap. Was woken from nap by planes (in Timberlea?); they were dropping water or fire retardant, I couldn't tell. Saw smoke plumes on the other side of Birchwood (Trails). There were news reports of two small fires.

Monday, May 2nd

Smoky in Timberlea; I thought the smell was Sunday's bacon. Went to work; the air was cleaner but the college shut the air intakes and we roasted in our offices.

Prairie Creek had been evacuated; funny stories from some affected coworkers. Auni and I roasted in the Recital Theatre that night for the One Acts Play Festival (a treat!); saw an eerie orange sun through a smoky plume as we went out for "fresh air" during intermissions.

Tuesday, May 3rd

It was a clear, blue-sky day. I said that over and over in the weeks following. I thought it was just another forest fire, now done. I was wrong.

Diane (active living devotee)

The story has been told many times about how we had two fires burning around Fort McMurray in the two days leading up to the evacuation. Like many others, we were accustomed to forest fires and had the false sense of security that our city would never burn. That it would never come that close. That the oil companies would come to our rescue or that our provincial firefighting crews would be mobilized and protect us.

We thought after Slave Lake, the lessons learned would never let something like that happen again.

Regardless, my family was somewhat prepared just in case. We had vehicles gassed up and ready to go. We had bags packed and I had staged some important items by the door for a quick grab and go. Not everything, but at least some belongings.

Katherine (quilter)

I'm surprised my cat still speaks to me.

Moped has always been a bit of a timid cat. When we moved to our current house, it took her a week to work up the courage to step outside. It was another week before she would venture off the deck.

In the years we have lived here, she has never tried to climb the back fence and on the rare occasion she has darted out the front door, she has never ventured off the front steps.

As the day of May 3rd progressed and both smoke and tensions mounted, Moped acted like nothing was amiss. Normally when I pull out a suitcase, her radar goes up and she follows me like a hawk or lays down in the suitcase. This time she just went about her usual cat naps and snacking. She barely took notice as I packed up her litter box and food.

Cyndy (composer)

Sunday, May 1, my husband Al and I sat in our lawn chairs in the back lane watching the water bombers. It was interesting and far removed from us.

We have lived in northern communities for most of our married life and forest fires are always a possibility. But they have always been remote possibilities—that is until noon hour, May 3.

Dee (poet)

While Fort McMurray had provided a good lifestyle for my family, our youngest was not thriving in school. By April we'd reached a point where we found a temporary option out of town, but we continued to hope and for a better solution.

While parked in Edmonton, my car was dented. Once back in Fort McMurray, I took my car to a garage to be repaired and insurance provided a rental.

My business was in a slump so I worked on various writing projects and kept my eye on the local job market for a suitable position from our home in the Timberlea neighbourhood of Eagle Ridge. My husband, Jeff, continued to work at one of the plants on a compressed work week, and was away at work. Our daughter, Chloe was living at home recovering from knee surgery and filling her days with work and volunteering as a Young Adults' leader, and our son Aaron was at his home asleep, resting between night shifts on a shutdown.

On May 2, I had prepared a double bed and two double foamies in case friends in Beacon Hill needed to evacuate their homes overnight.

My car had been in the shop for a week already, and since my husband and daughter both had vehicles I could borrow, I decided to return the rental Tuesday morning to avoid insurance overrun fees. The day was heating up.

The sky was blue, and the air had an earthy spring thaw fragrance. Typical to the area, we'd had a massive dump of snow just two weeks earlier, but now it was all melted and the Birchwood Trails had dried out from the intense sudden warming. The underbrush on the trails was dense and Conn Creek gurgled through the centre of the trails, as it trickled to the Athabasca River.

My husband and I were planning another trip to Edmonton for the following weekend. I texted my brother-in-law John, seeing if they were up for a visit. We were all set.

I headed to the Sawridge Hotel in Gregoire around 11 am, where the rental agency was based, my daughter promising to follow soon to give me a ride home. As I drove south over the bridge straddling the recently broken Athabasca River, I could see two thin columns of white smoke west of Beacon Hill. Nothing to worry about, I thought.

At the rental agency, about half an hour after I'd arrived, I followed an agent back out to the parking lot for a vehicle check. We both noticed a massive wall of black and grey smoke, and furious orange flames from behind the Burger King and the Beacon Hill Shell gas station.

"Wow, what happened? I thought it was under control?" I said.

We heard fire engine sirens and water bombers overhead. The forest fire would be under control again soon, I thought.

The agent snapped photos with his phone camera, and I hopped in my daughter's car as she pulled up next to me.

I snapped a photo of the fire as we drove by.

"How about coffee?" It was just before noon, and we seldom found time for mother-daughter coffee dates, but today we both had time.

Danelle (work-at-home mom)

Tuesday, May 3rd, 2016 started as a beautiful day. After a couple of days of evacuation notices, lots of smoke and even ash, Tuesday morning was a surprise. No smoke could be seen or smelled and the sun was shining bright.

Beacon Hill was put on a voluntary evacuation notice on Sunday, May 1st evening. I packed a few bags in case we had to go in the middle of the night. I felt we could have left without preparing if it was just us, but we had a five-month-old boy and a two-year-old little girl to think about.

Monday passed and was uneventful for our family. We kept watching the smoke from our back yard but didn't ever believe we were in direct danger.

Tuesday, 7:30 am, the kids were already anxious to get outside. Drew had left for work a few hours before. I packed the kids in the stroller and away we went on our much loved walk around Beacon Hill. We were on our second lap when Sadie begged to go to the park. We spent a little while there before heading to Saprae Creek for a play date with a good friend. I will be forever grateful for these memories. The day was quickly heating up but I still didn't notice any smoke when leaving the house around 9:45 am.

We had such a great time playing that I lost track of time and had to rush home for nap time. On the way back to Beacon Hill around 1 pm, I noticed something had changed.

There was a lot more smoke and it seemed closer than before. Still not feeling worried, I continued home and got the kids to sleep.

Michael (layperson)

Tuesday, May 3rd at approximately three o'clock in the afternoon, I was on my bed with my laptop typing away at a project. Living in the condos at the end of Riedel Street where it meets Prairie Loop Boulevard with my windows facing Downtown, I could see thick grey smoke which billowed from Abasand. Small specks of orange had begun to flicker through the tree line.

"Wow that's getting bad. They had better get a hold of that fire fast."

And yet, there was nothing in my mind screaming to pack and get ready to evacuate. I'd heard about certain areas being forewarned over the past couple of days (mostly about Prairie Creek), but assumed, as always, that the fire departments would get a handle on the situation. There've been forest fires around here most summers and they were always stopped, even when small evacuations (like Saprae Creek) had happened. In my mind, this wouldn't be any different.

Nevertheless, I took a moment to kneel down and pray for the city, the fire, and the people involved.

But then I was back to typing, believing it would be taken care of. Looking out the window from my third floor apartment, it did appear like those orange specks had disappeared.

David (firefighter with three sons)

I am a fire fighter in Fort McMurray. In early May, I was on days off and working on clearing (trees) in my back yard with a couple of guys at my home in Saprae Creek. The fire stretched from north to south on the west flank of the city, but there wasn't much cause for concern; forestry was taking care of it.

We were working and I could see the smoke from where I was in Saprae Creek. It was early afternoon when the wind changed.

All the heavy smoke started going over our heads. At that point I knew there was a problem.

Christina (public relations)

May 3rd

My husband is a firefighter and luckily he was on days off that week. We were at the park playing with our two boys and all the neighbourhood children that afternoon, when suddenly the wind changed.

We live in Abasand and so we had seen the flames burning in the distance for a few days now. But when the wind changed and the smoke changed colours my husband said for me to take the kids back to the house while he went to gas up his truck.

By the time he made it back from the Esso in Abasand we had received the mandatory evacuation notice.

PART III
THE FIRE

Jonathan (firefighter novelist)

May 3rd is a day I'll never forget. When it started, everything felt normal. Business as usual. I woke up early, enjoyed breakfast and kissed my pregnant wife goodbye for the day. The drive to work was a quiet and peaceful one, with no indication of what was to come – an event which would go into the books as one of the greatest trials in Fort McMurray history.

Throughout the morning of the 3rd, the city was calm, and it wasn't until around noon that things began to change. My partner and I were dispatched to a minor car accident that had occurred outside of the fire hall.

Approaching the scene, I was mesmerized by massive billowing smoke clouds that had seemed to materialize out of nowhere. It occurred to me that the accident may have been the result of distracted driving as even now, the sky was something almost indescribable. A sight hard to look away from.

The pillars of smoke were all encompassing, blocking out the western sky. With the angle of the sun behind the clouds, it looked as if the sky itself was on fire. I felt a sense of dread and unease at how large the smoke was and how close it looked

I suddenly noticed the number of people outside - whether gridlocked in traffic or standing on the streets staring up at the sky in awe; people were everywhere, just watching the smoke.

For a moment I stared as well, but soon my radio chirped, dispatching us to another medical call and I had to refocus on that. During the call downtown we listened anxiously to the radio, hearing our emergency dispatch sending fire trucks to Beacon Hill and Abasand.

The fire was here.

Diane (active living devotee)

The first thing that tipped me off that this was not a usual fire was the birds. When I went for my morning walk, they were leaving town. The sky was full of birds that looked like a black cloud moving north. The second thing was at the press conference when phrases like "drop in humidity", "fire crowning around noon", and "fire jumped the Athabasca" were mentioned. My husband used to be a firefighter. Those are not things you want to hear.

I had to go to the other side of town at 1:00 pm for my piano lesson. I spoke to my neighbour before I left, but there had been no new updates. The black smoke seen to the south had taken on an ominous red tinge. For me, this was the first time God showed up in this whole situation.

My daughter goes to school on the north side of town. As I crossed the river, I heard on the radio that the golf course was being evacuated. I could see the flames by the water treatment plant. I decided to skip my piano lesson and pick up my daughter instead. I wanted to miss the traffic in case they evacuated Thickwood. No thought to Beacon Hill at this point, it wasn't even mentioned.

By God's grace, traffic was still light but increasing in volume. I picked up my daughter at school and we headed south. Halfway home, we were notified by my husband that Beacon Hill was on fire and being evacuated. My daughter called my son to leave work and meet us at the house. I dread to think what would have happened if I hadn't picked her up when I did.

We may have been evacuated in different directions; I may not have been able to reach her. The thought leaves me shaking and weak. I'm profoundly grateful I listened to the small voice in my head that urged me to get her immediately and circumstances that had me heading north in the first place.

Once we reached home, the mad rush to load up the truck began. My son had to drive through the woods to get to us as the RCMP had closed access to Beacon Hill. We headed out and got stuck in traffic. The flames were everywhere.

Danelle (work-at-home mom)

I remember the radio saying it was still only a voluntary evacuation notice (for Beacon Hill) and people should not worry, but have your bags packed and ready.

I looked outside and saw an orange glow and black smoke very close. I called my husband, Drew, to let him know he should think about coming home and he wasn't sure he could because so many people were also getting calls and leaving.

The glow of the fire was getting worse so I decided to pack the car. I remember thinking it's no harm done, I may just have to unpack it later. Every time I brought something out of the house, the sky was getting darker and the glow, more ominous.

Neighbours started coming outside and I decided to get the kids and go. I called Drew to tell him he needed to come because we were leaving.

As he rushed to town, I grabbed Sadie out of bed, threw her Blankie and stuffed animals in her pillow case and rushed to the car. The radio still said only voluntary evacuation, but as I was strapping Sadie in, I heard a loud speaker going by saying "mandatory evacuation".

I ran back into the house, grabbed baby Jetlin (who was then crying hysterically, which started Sadie crying as well), and got him in the car.

The glow in the sky was worsening and I noticed it was 2:35 pm on the car's clock.

David (firefighter with three sons)

I got in touch with my wife, Jen, who was working at the hospital and she was quite distraught about everything because she'd heard about neighbourhoods in town being evacuated. I had the kids at home with me. I was looking after them, and I knew I would get called in to work, so I contacted one of our neighbours, Michelle, and she said she'd be able to look after the kids. She was in town, so there was a delay while she came back to Saprae. It gave me time to get the kids ready.

While I was doing that, a funny thing was that I took my camera and snapped photos around the house; just a precaution, in case there was a loss. I videoed the whole house. Actually, the previous summer, we'd been evacuated (so it was time I did it). I needed to be able to catalogue our house contents.

I took the memory card out of the camera and put it in my wallet, leaving the camera in the house. It was about 1 pm. So I dropped off the kids with Michelle. I wasn't overly concerned about the fire affecting us since it was pretty far from us at that point.

I headed in to Fire Hall No. 5, by Prairie Creek. The traffic was quite backed-up already past where the horse stables are, where they hold rodeos every year. I had to drive on the shoulder and got some rude looks.

I pulled into the fire hall and got into gear. There was one unit left, an older one, not much use—basically a moving tool box. We got on the air, the radio, and got our assignment to head up to Beacon Hill.

There was gridlocked traffic heading southbound out of Gregoire.

The police were very helpful in getting us through. We made our first stop in Beacon Hill and that was surreal with so much fire there.

We were assigned to help out the Bronto Crew, extending lines and protecting exposures and while that was happening, my wife was on the phone, trying to figure out what was happening with our children and figure out what she needed to do; she was quite concerned with all that was happening at the hospital.

Christina (public relations)

We went around our house (in Abasand) frantically putting things we thought we might need that night into a bag. I honestly still thought we would be coming back. My sister called and said she was stuck on the other side of town and asked if we could grab her dog at her house one street over.

All our neighbours were outside throwing things into vehicles. Our next door neighbour's husband couldn't make it home so we stayed to help her get her two kids loaded into their car.

Then we packed into our truck, our dog in his kennel, my sister's dog as well, and sat in gridlock traffic for nearly an hour just in front of our house.

I didn't start panicking until we saw a couple of houses catch and the water bombers flying overhead. I felt helpless... stuck.

Thomas (father to seven children)

I must've slept that night, because I woke to the alarm telling me it was time to get the kids ready for school. I looked to the west from the kitchen window. Everything looked calm, serene, and as it should be except for the mound of ash on the small deck we had. Breakfast made (cereal), lunches packed the night before, and everyone except the two smallest headed out for school.

All five older kids boarded one bus to the north side of the city to attend two different schools: four kids were heading to St. Paul's in Thickwood Heights, and the oldest to Holy Trinity Junior High in Timberlea.

Midmorning I got a text from the family friend explaining that she had slipped a disc in her back and wouldn't be able to help out with the kids. My shift was the next day.

Now what was I going to do? I told her not to worry about it, I would figure something out, and to get better.

Remembering that my lovely had promised friends of ours that I would repair the front door at the rental property they owned, I packed up my two babies and headed for the hardware store. It was 10 am.

By the time I found what I was looking for as a replacement door handle, the clock read 11 am. Good enough. I'll just pick up Zachy-boy from kindergarten at St. Paul's on the way. I texted the tenant to make sure this would be okay, and she assured me that she would play with the kids while I repaired the door. Good enough. Off we went.

I got to the house about noon after picking up a pizza for the three younger kids to munch on while I worked. We all met the tenant at the door, and as promised she scooted them out to the back to play with Bailey the St. Bernard-cross, and I got to work.

Fitting a new handle into the door, making adjustments, and finally satisfied with my work, I thanked the tenant for looking after the kids, and she happened to mention that she used to babysit. To my relieved surprise she agreed to look after the kids for a couple of days. Whew, two days covered so I can work my shift.

12:45 pm. Me and three of my kids were on the way south towards our home. I glanced to the west, and where it had appeared calm an hour earlier, the converse was true. Huge plumes of smoke covered the sky.

I wondered how much control was being maintained on this fire. In between country songs and radio ads I heard only, "Please remain calm, and shelter in place." We were supposed to stay inside. I kept watching the sky as we got closer to home. The smoke was getting worse and I was starting to get worried.

1:00 pm. The neighbour spies us pulling into our parking spot and waits as I park our faithful Yukon. He also happens to be the trailer park manager.

"Hi Jim," I start as I get out of the truck. I motion towards the clouds. "Whaddya think?"

"Well, we're going to head over to the old school if it gets any worse and wait it out there. Concrete structure, steel roof. We'd all be safe there. Just come on over whenever."

By this time the three younger ones had gotten out of the Yukon and were heading for the house to hopefully fill their little bellies with lunch. I hurried inside with them, and made the quickest hot dogs ever.

2:00 pm. The phone rings. It's my eldest at Holy Trinity, asking if it's okay to get a ride from a friend home, because the school is closing due to the fires. I agree, but please be safe, dear girl.

2:15 pm. The other school, St. Paul's calls, asking me to come pick up the kids. School is closing. I tell them I'm on my way.

2:17 pm. I'm standing outside, contemplating how to get this all done, when Jim hurriedly comes over and yells, "Mandatory evacuation! We have to get out in ten minutes!"

Alisa (engineer)

On Tuesday morning, May 3rd, I rode on a bus with my daughter's class on their field trip to the Discovery Centre. We finished the sessions there by 11:30 am and drove back past Beacon Hill, with no idea that a few hours later most of it would be gone. After my daughter went back to school, I slipped out of the house to get some groceries.

Inside Save On Foods (in Timberlea), it was eerie. At the check-out, the cashiers were chatting excitedly about evacuations. My daughter's school sent a text suggesting we pick up our kids.

Outside, during that one hour, the world had changed drastically. The entire eastern horizon was now one solid wall of black. The PetroCan across the street was lined up for blocks. The image of that gas station lineup filled me with horror. We didn't have enough gas in the city and the next fill-up was hundreds of kilometres away. If people were panicked over the basics, what would happen later?

I had worked on site for 10 years and was used to emergency situations. But out there, orders would be issued from a Command Post, and many different experts would respond. What experts would help us here in town?

Trish (storyteller)

Tuesday, May 3rd

The day went like this:

7:30 am

Went to Kal Tire for winter tire changeover; had breakfast skillet at McRae's while I waited. Someone who looked and spoke just like the fire chief also came in for breakfast and was relaxed and in a good mood. Tires done; went to work at the College.

2:00 pm

Black sky outside; message from College President to go home. Drove through town via Prairie Loop; saw hill above Grayling Terrace in flames. Sarah and Kevin said golf course is on fire.

On the bridge, saw flames on both sides of the Athabasca. Took 45 minutes to get home to Eagle Ridge from the College.

3:00 pm

Smoke plumes huge.

Phoned Dad (Qualicum Beach); listened to evacuation alerts on radio every two minutes. Texts passing in like crazy: where are you, when are you leaving.

Not until they say Timberlea.

Cokie (bird) is agitated. I see cars lined up on Loutit, both directions blocked. I am packing slowly over four-and-a-half hours before I see the order on CTV news.

Cyndy (composer)

Al had gone off to work as usual Tuesday morning. And I went to my regular Tuesday morning quilting club at my friend Sandra's house.

We ladies laughed, talked, prayed and quilted until noon. Then we parted. I hadn't left Sandra's driveway when Al called. "Get the fifth wheel ready. The fire has jumped the river." There was no evidence of impending doom, but I told Sandra the news and headed to Extra Foods (in Timberlea) to stock up the fifth wheel. I probably spent close to an hour in the store, trying to remain calm and not over-react.

I almost spoke to the check out lady about it, but didn't want to incite panic. So instead I wished her well and told her to stay safe.

When I left the store everything had changed. The air was acrid and above the ridge across Confederation Way the sky was black with smoke that rose to the heavens. I was stunned. I took a few pictures, hurriedly loaded my groceries and headed home.

My son Seth who worked in Gregoire as a mechanic called. "Mum! Get out now!"

Michael (layperson)

Not much longer, maybe 15 minutes, a massive pillar of blazing orange erupted from the corner of the hill overlooking the Hanging Stone River. The pillar must have been nearly 60 feet in the air and perhaps more. It raged forebodingly above the Grayling Terrace neighbourhood.

Immediately I was struck to the heart. One reason was that friends from our church family lived on the corner of Goodwin Place right where that orange pillar loomed.

My heart broke and I dropped to my knees pleading with the Lord for them. I prayed to the Lord who knows all that we are afflicted with that He would protect them. After all, they'd been through so much as a family, and in regards to their house specifically. Only a couple of years previously when the Hangingstone filled up, water had washed away all the trees behind their waterside home and threatened to tear away their backyard and collapse their house. Praise God, the waters abated and the city dropped in concrete blocks to hold the bank up which had receded all the way to the rear fence of their backyard.

"Please, Lord! Please spare them from this testing if it be your will!"

The second reason I began to pray through tears of anguish was this: "Lord, God, please do not wipe out this city! So many do not know you… please keep our city here so that we who know you can go on sharing the Gospel with those who do not!"

For 15 minutes I prayed and poured out my heart to our God who listens. But in His wisdom, the flames did not dissipate.

And yet, I still typed, assuming the flames would be put out, and content to flee only IF the flames leapt the highway into the downtown area.

I'd received a few texts from my mother starting at 3:14 pm, joking that her and my dad may need to crash at my place. She informed me that the fire had managed to jump the vast Athabasca and was now encroaching upon Thickwood Heights where they lived near Westwood High School, and that Thickwood was now added to the list of areas under mandatory evacuation.

I actually replied via text: "Oh no… That's insane. Ok I'll get the bedding ready" and then immediately followed that up with "Actually, let me know closer to 6 pm. I'm working on my project. What about Melissa and Ryan and the kids?" referring to my sister and her fiancé and their children who also lived in Thickwood and near the tree line by Signal Road.

I truly anticipated that everything would be under control shortly. I'd even texted to her in reply to her saying she packed poorly, "All I'd bring is my Bible and my laptop. Everything else can be replaced. It appears that somehow the fire has burned itself out on the other side of the highway downtown"

The giant pillar had subsided, although there was some fire in the trees on the high bank coming down from Beacon Hill to the Hangingstone (River). But it was back to work on the project.

Then I got this text from my sister at 4:31 pm: "Where are you? the radio says the whole city has to evacuate"

Surprised I replied, "To where?"

"Noralta Grey Wolf Lodge," she answered.

"Ok" was my quick response.

"Have you packed yet?" she added.

"Nope. But I will now." And so then with some sense of urgency, I saved what I'd added to my project and shut down the word processor.

I posted this prayer to Facebook:

"Please pray this prayer. There is only one God. He is the God of creation. He is sovereign over all. Only He has the power to quench this fire. Only He has the power to save us both mortally and eternally. Please, whether you believe or not, humbly believe, and pray:

Heavenly Father, you are the God above all gods. Only to you does creation bow. You are forgiving and you are merciful. We know that we grieve you in our sin. We confess that we do not put you in the right place of authority, nor do we give you the attention you deserve with this life you have blessed us with. Please have mercy on us. Please spare our homes. Please permit us just a little more time to work and live here so that you may be glorified and receive the glory you deserve. Please protect and help those fighting this fire. Give them wisdom with how to respond. But please God, open up the heavens and bring rain. I trust that you are good no matter what you allow to happen. Your will be done.
"We ask this in Jesus' Name;
Amen"

As my mother's texts had suggested, I listened to the radio. I then found Country 93.3 FM online and started to stream it, hoping for updates.

Song after song played as I grabbed a laundry bin, put my Bible in it, the little preserved food I had (a couple of puddings, some granola bars), and some bags of mini Caramilk pieces from Youth Group. I understood that at this time, as always, God would be working in peoples' hearts. Children would need to experience the reassuring love of God through the simple gift of a candy. And knowing that people would need the hope Christ offers, I added various stacks of gospel tracts to the laundry bin.

I wasn't sure how things would play out, but I envisioned myself inviting people to pray, forming a prayer circle, and praying for God to intervene on our behalf with a torrential downpour. Often it is at the bleakest moment when God shows up in order to respond to prayer and prove that he is there, listening, waiting for his children to call upon him, so that he may answer and display his power over creation.

In my finite mind, I did not understand how God would be working. I could only expect one response, but in any case I knew he was intimately invested in what was happening around us.

I had a quick shower, brushed my teeth, and jumped into a clean pair of clothes. I brought only one clean change of underwear and socks, because naturally, this would all be handled and resolved in the next three days and we'd be back home. I could handle being in something slightly soiled for 72 hours. I've been through worse while in the Canadian infantry.

Looking back to the 93.3 FM stream, I was puzzled as to why songs were playing and no one was giving us instructions. Finally, an automated evacuation message came on instructing people downtown to go north and I realized the station had been abandoned and this message was set to play after every three or four songs.

Recognizing that the Lord gives and the Lord takes away, I scanned my apartment. None of it was really important. None of it could I take into the grave and into Heaven to be with God himself. No pictures and memories that I could cling to until my mortal life ended would go with me either. No good thing in this life would compare to what lay ahead with Jesus Christ in eternity.

His word contained in the Holy Bible would see me and others through in this time of trial. My laptop which contained all of my ministry work as well as possible plans for God's work in the future needed to be saved as well. I'd spent nearly four years preparing an online ministry to help people know the God who created them and loves them. I did not want to lose such things.

I also knew that if God desired to take away my home and all my possessions, there would be great purpose in it that I may not yet understand, but that if I was faithful in trusting him, I would receive joy.

Truly, although my trust was fully in God, I recognized that if I really felt I needed some of my belongings back, I would be able to claim them through insurance. But was there anything I did not wish to have to try and replace? Yes, my firearms, one of which was custom built.

I packed up the few pieces I owned in two long-barrel cases, locked them, and then moved everything downstairs to my car. Problem was, the cases were too long for my trunk. And

I'd be a fool to put them in my backseat as I'd be unable to leave them there at the camp I was to evacuate to. Any thief looking through the back window could easily smash in and steal them.

So I left my laundry bin of goods in the backseat and rushed the guns back upstairs to return them to the gun-safe. Time was being eaten up. I wasn't panicked, but I understood that time was almost literally burning away.

Dee (poet)

"The fire looks pretty bad. Let's go somewhere and have a better look," Chloe said. The radio was on, and we heard an announcer report that fire crews were on the scene, but the fire was moving quickly now, and had jumped the Athabasca River. We were stunned.

As we drove north over the Athabasca River, I videotaped the fire in the distance, westward from the bridge. The trees were engulfed on the south side behind Abasand Heights, as well as on the north side of the river, near the Fort McMurray Golf Club.

"I can't believe it," was all I could say. How could the fire have grown so large, so quickly? I loaded the video onto Twitter as I was in the habit of using social media for business promotion. My hands shook a little, overcome by the scene. There was now a mandatory evacuation of Beacon Hill, we heard on the radio.

Chloe drove us through heavy but quickly moving traffic to Abraham, a parcel of land under development between Thickwood Heights and Timberlea. We got out of the car while continuing to listen to volunteer and then mandatory evacuation notices.

"I doubt it will affect us," I said.

"We better go home and pack, just in case," Chloe said. "I'll drop you off to get started, and I'm going to fill up the car with gas." I wasn't sure why filling up with gas was necessary, but she had quite a lot of emergency training so I didn't question her.

Having just finished reading the novel, All The Light We Cannot See, by Anthony Doerr, I decided to fill the bathtubs in our home with water, just in case our services were cut off, as the water treatment plant is located next to the Fort McMurray Golf Club. When my daughter returned, she told me to fill jugs and pitchers with drinking water, which I did.

My husband phoned and asked how things were in town; several of his coworkers with young families had to rush home to calm their panicking wives and pack for evacuation. I updated him, but reassured him that things were fine. I was fine. We shouldn't need to evacuate; I was ready for guests and I would pack a few things, just in case. He asked me to snap photos of the contents of our house, as a precaution. And he considered whether or not to work overtime, as his department would be short-staffed.

Social media went crazy with panicking mothers, desperate for direction on what to do, where to go. There were some sensible replies, so I avoided going online, but I texted my brother-in-law about how crazy things were getting.

"Come today," he texted back.

It sounded like a good idea. With our planned trip to Edmonton later in the week, it sounded like a good idea to get out of town while the fire was causing so much panic, I thought.

When my husband phoned from work, I said, "No, don't work overtime. Come home. We can head to Edmonton together."

"This fire is causing a lot of panic. Everyone is leaving. I'm coming home on the early bus," he said.

I resisted the urge to get into a vehicle and head south right away. I needed to wait for my husband to return from work, around 5 pm. I decided to pack weekend suitcases for myself and my husband. Our youngest was already safely out of town with his own things, so I didn't need to worry about him.

We played a local radio station loudly, so we could hear it as we worked.

Heavy dark smoke blocked the sky as the afternoon wore on in a blur.

My neighbour was outside in her backyard, turning on sprinklers.

"We did this in the Okanagan," she said.

"Embers blowing onto roofs were the cause of many houses burning down there, not the fire directly," added her husband.

"If it jumped the Athabasca, I doubt a sprinkler will stop the fire," I told her. The gentle tinkle of water seemed grossly inadequate. Yet, her anxiousness set off my own, and I began to wonder: what if the fire does spread to us? The wall of smoke and flames seemed to be getting closer behind us, beyond the Birchwood Trails. I went back inside to see what else to do.

I texted with several friends who were in various stages of packing, leaving their homes, driving past flames, confused about heading north to work camps, or south to Edmonton.

"We have room; come over here." I still doubted we'd need to leave, but since we were going out of town, people could at least stay in our home. I put some laundry into the washing machine and checked our food supply. I planned what I could cook for dinner for a crowd.

The radio called for mandatory evacuations for Thickwood, Wood Buffalo, Dickinsfield. A friend sent me a photo of trees on fire in Dickinsfield, just across the Birchwood Trails from our house. There was also fire reported in Timberlea, on Tower Road, just two neighbourhoods west of us.

Panic did ripple through me then. I put the sprinkler on in our backyard, and thought about the cushions on the patio furniture. What if an ember landed on a chair by the house, and as a result, the house burned down? I unfastened the cushions and tossed them down off the deck. With thickening smoke and raining ash, I began to wonder if our lives were in danger.

I put the wet washed clothing into the clothes dryer while deciding to send an email to our youngest's school, to let them know family contacts in Edmonton, just in case we didn't make it. I cc'd our relatives, letting them know how to contact our son's school. I wasn't sure what would happen, but I wanted to cover all the bases.

John, and then our nephew's wife Melissa texted, to check on the situation. I looked around at our home and belongings and I wasn't concerned. It was all just stuff. Documents could be replaced, and I had lots of photos on social media which meant I didn't need to haul my files or photo albums around.

In the laundry room, I folded the last of the laundry and added a few items to my packing. Watching the smoke and flames beyond the trails through the window, I noticed two men, renters next door, watering their backyard. I went outside and told them, "You'd better pack. We'll probably be evacuated." They were surprised and went off to gather their belongings.

A friend texted and said she was heading to a northern camp. But they were filling up; maybe they'd have to camp outside.

Gas stations were lined up. Some had run out of gas. Traffic was building, and schools were letting children go home. Inside again, my daughter noticed that I was scatter-brained, not focusing on anything in particular.

"Focus, Mom," she said. "We'll have to take the pets. And camping gear, in case there's nowhere to stay."

"Okay. Let's gather pet supplies." We began to move things to the garage, making a pile to take: our overnight bags, drinking water, camping gear, dry food, pet food, the youngest's lizard in a smaller terrarium, our portable electronics including my ancient laptop. My daughter added some of her outdoor equipment to the pile, such as her avalanche beacon.

My phone rang: "Mom, why didn't you phone me?" My son Aaron had been woken by his girlfriend, Aryn. She'd insisted that he get up and pack, as now the evacuations were mandatory everywhere except Timberlea. Aryn had evacuated in the Okanagan before, so she wanted to be ready.

"Sorry, Son. I thought we'd be okay here. We aren't under evacuation. Come over. You can stay here." I continued to invite friends and my sister; I had a place for them to sleep and food to feed everyone.

Once my son Aaron came over, the radio stations became unmanned as announcers had to go home and pack. We turned on the television to find Fort McMurray on the news.

The Beacon Hill Shell was ablaze. The entire neighbourhood was engulfed. It couldn't be.

My son ate while I fielded more texts, too nervous to eat.

Around 5 pm, a loud siren came from the TV. A mandatory evacuation order for all of Fort McMurray. Now it became real. We had to leave.

We loaded the vehicles. I would drive my husband's yellow truck with our boy's Sheltie puppy, O'Malley; Chloe would drive her car with the Bearded Dragon, Stubbs, and Aaron had his Lab-cross, Cay.

The sky was black to the south and west. Ash rained down on us. The air was thick with smoke, making it difficult to breathe. My sister texted to let me know she was being diverted north, even though she'd been driving to my house. I silently prayed that everyone would escape safely.

As we pulled away from the house, I thought it might not be there when we returned. I couldn't see beyond that; just that the house could be burned up and there was nothing we could do.

The account of Job in the Bible crossed my mind: Satan had approached God, mocking and sneering that God had blessed and protected Job. As a result, God had allowed Satan to test Job.

Would Job be faithful to God, even if Satan removed all his material possessions, even the lives of his children?

JD (radio announcer & reporter)

Tuesday May 3rd, around 11 am I went to a press conference with Darby Allen (the Fire Chief). I'd been to two press conferences the day before as well--one in the morning, and one in the afternoon. This press conference was with Darby Allen and the emergency response folks who were gathered at the Fire Station on Airport Road.

We heard from Darby, the Mayor (Melissa Blake), and from the Alberta Forestry folks about the current situation. I will never forget the words that Darby Allen said.

Darby said, "Today is going to be ugly."

We looked around, and it was a beautiful day; there wasn't any smoke around, and he said it was going to be ugly. Well... so the sore feeling in my stomach broadened quite a bit at that point.

I got back to the (radio) station, left again for another drive around town (at lunch), and returned to the station at about 12:40 pm. I was to be on the air for the mid-day show between 1 and 4 pm. Just before I went on the air, I went outside just one more time to take a look, and I saw the first major plumes of smoke coming out straight ahead (west) of me, from the Beacon Hill area.

My stomach really turned at this point. I realized the severity of the situation, but at the same time, it was hard to believe what I was seeing. I ran back into the station. My show was no longer going to be about what I had planned, but about preparing for the situation: what documents to have, what to take (during evacuation).

I went out of the station every 15 to 20 minutes and saw the situation get progressively worse. From where I stood, I could see Waterways to my left, Beacon Hill in front of me, and Abasand Heights to the right. I saw the three main (affected) areas surrounding me.

My co-worker came back to the station to take over, so I could attend the press conference planned for 4 pm at City Hall. Well, that wasn't going to happen as I got into my car and hit gridlocked traffic.

After about a half hour of maneuvering through parking lots, I circled back to the station. My coworker had to leave to be with her children, as her husband was going to need to be up in a helicopter soon (as pilot). I was in the radio station until we were told to leave.

Before that happened, I had a few moments when I needed to step outside to get some fresh air, which turned out to be smoke-infused. I phoned my sister in Rocky Mountain House and asked her and the rest of my family there to pray for me, as I was feeling on the verge of a panic attack.

My sister prayed for me, for comfort, and that God would help us through that situation and get out of the city alive. After she prayed, I felt this incredible sense of peace that I have never felt before, draped over me. I was given clarity of mind, energy and strength to go back on the air. I have never felt that kind of Holy Spirit energy before.

Back inside, I got a call from my friend, Alix at Dunvegan Gardens (on Draper Road), who was absolutely overwhelmed, in tears, freaking out.

"We are surrounded by fire! We're not going to be able to get out of this alive. We're gonna die. We're surrounded by fire. There's nowhere for us to go. The road is blocked, the boat we have to head down the (Clearwater) river is out of gas, we are stuck, we are stranded. We are going to die."

The only thing I could do in that moment was pray. That's all I could do. So I prayed, "Lord, protect Alix, protect the family at Dunvagen Gardens--Brad and Terri Friesian and their family, all of their workers, employees, the families of those employees, the customers, all the people who live down Draper (Road), and in Waterways."

That was all I could do in that moment. There was nothing more. All I could do was pray. As it turns out, that was the most I could do; that is what was necessary for that situation.

Firefighters from the fire station down the road from us came and told us we needed to leave at 4:30 pm. We did our final goodbyes on the air, not knowing if we'd be able to come back again.

For some reason, I had it in my heart that I was going to die. I was convinced that I was there to give information to the public, to help the public get through, but that I was going to die at the station. I thought this was my final act of helping others on the earth.

I walked outside and saw fire from all sides. I was one hundred percent convinced that I was a goner, going down with the ship.

My boss and I left the station and drove up to Franklin Ave and we were re-routed to Hospital Street. Abasand was completely on fire. I lived in Abasand for my first nine months in Fort McMurray, so I had a very personal connection to that neighbourhood. It was overwhelming. We were operating out of adrenaline slowly making our way in heavy traffic north from downtown, up Highway 63.

I told my boss that I would really like to get to my house to get a few things. Confederation Way was backed-up with a lot of traffic. What would normally take us five minutes, turned into a half hour drive.

As we were driving west toward Eglert Drive, vehicles were driving toward us on the wrong side. All four lanes were taken by people driving toward the highway. It was absolutely terrifying. I thought we were going to have a head-on collision.

Elizabeth (artist)

May 3rd was a beautiful, sunny warm day. Nothing seemed out of the ordinary. I was just about to prepare to get ready for work when I looked out my 4th floor apartment window. I noticed that there was backed up traffic on one of the main roads leading to one of the families I work for. I do respite work for families.

I called my client to mention that I might be late today because there was traffic backed up on Confederation Drive. She told me that she was in the process of packing to evacuate in her area of Wood Buffalo because the fire was close to her home. So I went on the balcony and looked towards Abasand Heights. I saw a large pillar of smoke going up in the sky.

I called my sister, in Eagle Ridge to see if she'd heard anything. My sister told me that other areas where being evacuated, and she had prepared a room for evacuees from other parts of the city and she was not expecting her area to be evacuated. She suggested that I go over to her home and we could sit it out together and have supper.

Since my area was not yet being evacuated, I decided I should pay my rent. I had tried a couple of days ago, but the debit machine had been down. I was worried I would lose my apartment if I did not pay it.

I noticed that there was also backed up traffic in front of my apartment building, so I decided to walk as the office was only a few blocks from my home.

The air was smoky and very warm. Traffic was bumper-to-bumper. When I got to the corner gas station, I noticed that many people were trying to fill up with gas. Some people were getting frustrated and trying to fight to get in to the gas station ahead of others.

When I reached the rental office and the doors were locked, I thought the fire situation must be serious if no one was in the office. So I walked back to my apartment at a faster pace though I had a peace that the Lord was with me.

I packed a suitcase and put it in my car along with a bottle of water. It was hot and I didn't know how long I would be in my car. I turned my radio to the local station to hear if we were going to be evacuated soon, while driving to my sister's home, which should have taken five minutes. I heard we were not in mandatory evacuation yet so I was at ease.

It took me an hour to get to the Confederation Way intersection. By then the voluntary evacuation had turned mandatory.

Joe (RCMP & Harley rider)

I was working in the RCMP District office in St. Paul; I had been seconded to a position for an indeterminate amount of time and was travelling back and forth to my home in Lloydminster each day. I was just getting ready to make the drive home when my supervisor asked me to wait, saying that we might have to go to Fort McMurray.

We had a quick meeting and a conference call and loaded up whatever supplies we thought we might need. I always carried a "go bag" when I worked in case I had to suddenly overnight somewhere; just a few necessities and some extra clothes to get by for a couple of days.

It was late in the day when I finally began to make the journey to Fort McMurray. I took Highway 881 from Lac La Biche and on one of my stops posted to FaceBook, "Driving to Fort McMurray on Highway 881. Yes TO. Makes me sad to see so many families fleeing from their home." (I never expected such an overwhelming response and I became a bit emotional when I read through the responses.)

Traffic was a steady stream and moving quite slowly. Vehicles littered the highway and ditches in Anzac; the service station a sea of vehicles and people as I drove by.

When I arrived at the Highway 881–Highway 63 junction, traffic fleeing the city was at a standstill and occupied all four lanes including the northbound flow which had been used to double the flow away from the city.

I waited at that point for one of my St. Paul colleagues to arrive and once he did, we travelled along the shoulder into the city.

Vehicles that had run out of fuel had been abandoned on the shoulders and in the ditches. The scene was apocalyptic, unbelievable and devastating.

PART IV
ESCAPE

Joe (RCMP & Harley rider)

I lived and served with the RCMP in Fort McMurray for eight years transferring out in 2014. We left behind my son and one of my stepdaughters. I remember getting a call early on May 3rd from my stepdaughter who was trying to drive out and was somewhere near Beacon Hill.

I heard the panic in her voice and could visualize what she was seeing. She said she was going to burn up, but I told her to just keep going and she would soon be out of the area. I think she needed someone to just be on the phone with her to comfort her and encourage her to keep going.

Thomas (father to seven children)

I quickly strap the three youngest kids into Vincent the Van now, and run inside, grabbing the laundry basket in the hallway and scooping up whatever clothes I can find for the kids and myself, remembering to grab the package of marriage and birth certificates on the way.

Tops of dressers cleaned off, diapers, wipes, a few bottles of water, some snack bars and I run back outside. I hear explosions behind me as I run for the van, literally tossing the basket of whatever clothes into the trailer, praying the three kids have decided to behave and are still in their seats. Thankfully, they are.

As I start the engine, the radio comes to life and the first thing I hear is that the main road through town is now blocked due to fire. This is a huge problem. Four of my kids are on the north side of that fire, the oldest heading to a friend's home, and the three younger at St. Paul's. I'm on the south side of the city!

Not caring if any cop sees 'Distracted Driving' while using my phone, I frantically dial St. Paul's as I put Vincent the Van into gear. Trying to be polite, and after informing her that the road is now impassable, I ask the principal what is going to happen to my three kids.

A brief pause and then, "Mac Island! They're going to Mac Island! I have to go, it's very busy in here!" And then CLICK, the line is dead.

I am being forced to leave four of my children on the north side in a wildly burning city with strangers, three enroute to MacDonald Island Downtown, and one at her friend's home in Timberlea. And I can do absolutely nothing about it. I promised them safety.

Tears are trying to force their way into my eyes, and I blink them away just as forcefully. I don't have time for that right now. I have to think, think, think! Please try to think, I tell myself. What can I do? What can I possibly do to save my kids?

Reason re-enters my mind as the tears are forced away and I start going through a mental list of people I know in this city. People that know my kids, and know how much I love them. Renee, Hugh, Mike, Sasha, Barry, Glen... the list grows, and I have numbers for all of them.

I start texting, imploring them to look out for my kids as they get to Mac Island. Please! Every single one promises to, and assures me they will be cared for. I can do nothing else for those three beautiful children. I have to leave. The police are making me leave! I'm so sorry, babies! I have to go!

I don't want to go south, everything in me screams to go north, fight through the fire and find my kids. Then I look in the rear view mirror and see three more beautiful children, obliviously trusting their Daddy to take them to safety.

They are quiet and wide-eyed as we drive past a field completely engulfed in flame, trees exploding from the intense heat, and as I look in the side view mirror I see just how dangerously close those flames are to the trailer we are pulling.

Accepting that this is the way things must be at the moment, I text my oldest daughter, also with an almost complete stranger, encouraging her to be brave, to keep a clear head, and that I will find her.

I promise myself that I will find them, I will have all of them back, and I will not stop until I do. I pray for my kids, asking God to protect them, asking for angels to guard them. Just as I finish, the phone rings.

It's my wife; my lovely, beautiful, cruise-shipping wife.

"Hi, sweetheart" I begin.

She is near panic, "What's going on?! I just got a call from the school asking me to come pick up the three kids at Holy Trinity! Fort McMurray is on fire?"

Miracle number one. My lovely's cruise ship had drifted into cell range at the right time to tell me that my three kids were being taken from St. Paul's to Holy Trinity, and not Mac Island, as Downtown is now unsafe.

As her call starts to fade, I tell my lovely that we are evacuating, and I don't know where the kids are, but I will find them.

The other line starts ringing. It's the tenant from earlier in the day, the one I've met twice, ever. Time for miracle number two.

"Are you okay? Is there anything I can do to help?" She's on the north side of the city, close to my kids. Very close.

I choke back heart-bursting tears as I say, "I need someone to pick up my kids at Holy Trinity!"

She assures me she will, and then her call also fades. Cell towers are burning now, or overloaded, leaving Fort McMurray in a communications blackout. I put my phone down, and suddenly there is peace. I don't know where my kids are, but I know who will take care of them.

We are in an immense line of traffic, leaving Fort McMurray with thousands of other people. Surprisingly, and oh so thankfully, no one panics. The exodus is orderly and everyone gets out safely to Anzac and points south, or so we thought.

Diane (active living devotee)

The flames were everywhere. This is when my eighteen-year-old became my hero. In one moment, he left his childhood behind and stepped fully into manhood. He stayed in contact with me via cell phone and told me to put the truck in four wheel drive.

He led in his 4Runner and I stayed close to his bumper. He led us down the embankment in Beacon Hill. It didn't take long for others to follow us.

We spilled out onto the highway. People let us into the southbound lanes that resembled a parking lot not a highway.

I got scared as the fire rolled over the highway and the world went black.

I remember everything being hot, red and black.

I remember asking God if this was how I would die; on the highway.

Through it all, my son (over the phone) calmly talked me through, telling me to follow him, not to look out the side windows, don't lose him and he would get us out.

He led us over the median, up the hill by United Furniture Warehouse, past burning trees and into Gregoire. We took a winding route through the subdivision to make sure his girlfriend and her family got out.

We finally exited out by the industrial park on Highway 69 and headed south to our meet up location by the gun club.

Danelle (work-at-home mom)

Traffic lined Beacon Hill Drive. I spoke with Drew, letting him know we weren't moving. I inched forward and finally got to a spot where I could see through to the trees on the west side of Beacon Hill. They were already burning.

I told Drew I didn't think I could get out because the fire was already engulfing the only entrance/exit; that I had to go over the berm to get to highway 63.

As soon as I saw an opening in traffic, I hopped the curb and got to the top of the berm. I wanted to make sure I couldn't get out on the road before risking going through the ditch because I saw one vehicle was already stuck.

With Drew on speaker phone and trying to keep the kids calm, I realized the fire was already burning into Beacon Hill and I couldn't go back to Beacon Hill Drive. Drew told me he couldn't get to us in time and had to turn around.

Sadie saw the flames and yelled "Mommy! Mommy! The fire!"

I had no idea how to calm her down but I told her "it's okay, Sweetheart. Jesus might decide to take us to Heaven and that's okay. He is taking care of us and he will decide what happens".

I kept telling Drew that I needed him to know I loved him because we might not make it out.

With prayer and Drew's guidance, I made it into and out of the ditch and onto highway 63. Visibility was almost zero but there were police officers still directing traffic as we got through the intersection of Beacon Hill Drive and Highway 63.

Later I learned they were pulled from the area only minutes after we got through; the highway closing to southbound traffic soon after.

The fire had crossed the highway and was starting to burn the trees bordering Gregoire. We drove through thick black smoke with flames surrounding us for less than a minute but it seemed like forever.

Centennial Trailer Park was burning (on the right) as we passed. I remember thinking I was so grateful for the inner air circulation button in the car along with air conditioning. It was 31°C outside.

Once we passed through the smoke, I noticed a man had stopped on the side of the highway and was extinguishing a fire that had started under the hood of his truck while driving through.

I decided we needed to keep going south to be safe and Drew said he would come when he could. I was so worried about him staying north, but my priority was keeping the kids safe.

Being the awesome husband he is, Drew had filled up the gas tank the day before. We were blessed to be in one of the first waves of people leaving so the highway wasn't busy. I was still nursing Jetlin so had to pull over at times to feed him. The kids travelled surprisingly well and seven hours later we arrived at a friend's house, our safe haven.

I had kept 'it' together all along until we arrived and Sadie said, "Mommy, I miss Daddy".

I was able to say "Me too, Sweetie," before bursting into tears. I'm so thankful our friends were there to offer support.

David (firefighter with three sons)

My wife Jen was evacuated north, up to one of the camps. Her brother was up there, so she met up with him. The kids were still with Michelle in Saprae Creek.

I got bounced around to help fight fires in different spots. From Beacon Hill I went Downtown, and then we got moved up to Thickwood and fought a house fire there. Fortunately, we were able to contain the Dickinsfield fire to just a couple of houses.

Next we moved to Wood Buffalo to protect one of the big apartment buildings. There's a slough behind there—marshland. We couldn't get our hoses in there, so pretty much stomped most of it out and splashed water up onto the fire. My boots filled with water which turned out to be pretty bad as I got nasty blisters from having wet boots.

Trish (storyteller)

7:30 pm

Gridlock trying to get out of Timberlea via Parsons Creek. Cokie (my bird) is in cage screeching.

SHUT UP.

Smoke is getting closer. I see distant flames. I am going to die in Timberlea. STOP CRYING. I have to pee--NOW. They are only letting us go north on Hwy. 63.

I pee under the Parsons Creek overpass. Traffic crawling along.

COKIE, SHUT UP FOR THE LOVE OF GOD.

9:00 pm

Sun is setting. Traffic is still crawling. No local radio. CBC Edmonton says go to Noralta Lodge. Where is that? Warren says Noralta is full.

Auni is waiting in a long line at Syncrude. Where are all these other work camps?? They keep listing them and I don't know any.

I am alone and the bird is screeching. SHUT UP COKIE.

10:30 pm

Sun sets and Cokie shuts up. People are pulling over everywhere to camp. Frogs are loud at Crane lake; car still says 28 degrees; air is hot.

I keep crawling on. Amalis (Victoria) texts to say she has boy troubles. NOT NOW AMALIS.

11:00 pm

Linda is at Shell; I will head there. Then Auni calls; she, Warren, and Ermias made it to CNRL Joslyn.

She tells me to ignore the lady with the Firebag sign; turn left instead at Fort McKay. 19 km more; no cars; going fast now.

Then I'm lost. Auni? Not responding. Warren? He picks up and talks me in. Auni meets me and signs me in at the office; seems I cannot read or write.

Joslyn staff are calm; the place is calm, quiet. They take me in, give me a room, towel, soap. Out of danger.

1:30 am

Finished talking to folks on phone. Finish catching up with Auni.

Text Amalis to acknowledge her boy issues and explain the delay in my reply. Go to bed.

Katherine (quilter)

While the packing had gone smoothly, it was with trepidation that I carried her through the shower of burnt pine needles and put her in the truck. Like most cats, Moped is not fond of car rides. As soon as she is put in a vehicle she starts to cry and does not stop until we arrive at our destination (the vet's office). How would she handle this ride? Would she cry the WHOLE way? What if she got car sick?

Maybe the slow pace of the truck fooled her into thinking we weren't moving. Maybe she could somehow sense that this trip was different. Maybe it was part of the divine intervention that was so widespread that day.

Moped barely made a peep as my husband slowly drove north for six hours to Syncrude. As we sat parked on Confederation Way, we even opened the door to her cage. She just lay with her head far enough out to see around her and remained quite content with her situation.

Syncrude had opened its doors to employees; however, their camp had been closed for several months.

The staff made a huge effort to get it as ready as they could on such short notice. Moped, my husband and myself shared a small room with a single bed (without bedding), one chair, cold water in the communal bathrooms and a layer of grit on everything.

I have never been so thankful and felt such 'survivor's guilt' over having so much more than those we had passed on the side of the road and much of the world for that matter. After hiding in the closet for a while getting used to the dogs barking next door and the frequent traffic in the hall, Moped claimed the one chair in the room as her own. She graciously left the bed for us.

The next afternoon we packed up again and headed to Albian. I don't think Moped or I will ever forget the experience, but for far different reasons. While the hustle and bustle of the Albian camp foyer represented help, resources and eventual escape to me, it was a little different for Moped.

For a cat not used to being around more than eight people at a time, the hundreds milling around was overwhelming. Large dogs kept coming up to sniff her cage. After the third person asked if we had a cat or a dog, I looked in the cage to find she had buried herself under a towel. We began referring to it as the 'Towel of Safety' and she hid under it anytime the situation became too much for her.

We checked in to stay the night. We now had a larger room, a double bed with pillows and blankets, access to a cafeteria and tables handing out toiletries, pet care items, etc. Everything you could need. No questions asked. I give a special shout out to whoever thought of having cat litter on hand.

That night, Moped had reached her limit. Ever since we adopted her as a kitten, she has tried to eat my hair. Even though I have never permitted it, this is still how she tries to comfort herself. Knowing that the direct approach would not work, she jumped up on the end of the bed, walked between the wall and my sleeping husband, across the top of his head to mine and started chewing.

I moved her or put her on the floor. This would last a few minutes and then start again. All night long.

The next day we boarded a bus to head to the airstrip. Moped failed to appreciate that this represented another major step in 'getting out'. Rather than enjoying the time with fellow travelling companions that included dogs, lizards and whatever else lived in those cardboard boxes, she spent her time trying to get between my back and my seat. Even the Towel of Safety was of minimal comfort. She then got to take her first plane trip. Thanks to the lenient pet policies in place, she was able to travel in the cabin behind the last row of seats.

We were greeted in Edmonton by my in-laws. All of us were spent. Moped had not eaten or had anything to drink for many hours. In the car we took the top off of her cage.

Initially I was concerned about having a cat loose in the car. I needn't have worried. She just lay there like a puddle of melted ice cream all the way to Elk Point.

Cyndy (composer)

My son Seth who worked in Gregoire as a mechanic called. "Mum! Get out now! Don't stop for anything. Get the kids and leave town now!" He said he was coming across the bridge to help me collect the children but the traffic was crazy.

I told him I would get Faith and I'd ask our son-in-law Joel to pick up Jared at the Christian School because it was close to his house.

Faith arrived home before I could go for her. I guess they were dismissing school early. I had a half of a tank of gas. The gas station was a mad house.

Every road was lined with cars waiting on the pumps. We sat in line for a long time. Finally, I was able to nose in. The guy who let me in was gracious. I gassed up and we headed out of town, going south to Edmonton.

The traffic was thick, but I remember being impressed that people were driving in an orderly fashion. No honking, no road rage.

Our daughter Patience who worked at the golf course had called to say that the place was on fire. The staff was evacuating. She could see the wall of flames bearing down on them.

The sky was thick with smoke; Abasand was on fire.

We crossed the Athabasca River. The traffic was slow by now. I knew that Joel was ahead of us with Jared.

Patience was somewhere behind me in her CR-V. We were keeping in touch by phone. She was afraid.

Downtown was unearthly and bizarre. Regular traffic was non-existent. Police officers were waving people through traffic lights.

The smoke hung low like thick fog. I remember being grieved for the emergency workers who were operating in that soup. Some had a handkerchief over their nose and mouth but most didn't. I wondered if they were terrified as they stayed behind so we could get out. If they were, they certainly never showed it.

We reached the last cross-street before Beacon Hill and I realized they were turning us back. I didn't know why, but they told us to turn around and go north. I pulled over to the side.

I called Patience to let her know. I told her not to panic but to follow me once she was turned around. I would wait for her.

The next thing I knew she was calling back, crying. They had pushed her through.

I guess when I got to that spot the fire had jumped the highway. By the time she got there, the fire had crossed the highway behind her and so they ordered her to continue south. She could only think that we were trapped in the fire and she was nearly hysterical.

I assured her we were okay and told her to go up the road, meet up with her brother and brother-in-law. We would all try to get to her sister Rose's farm near Winfield.

Faith and I continued north.

I called Al and he told me he was on his way home. He had managed to snag a ride with a coworker who had his own vehicle. He would be home in 40-50 minutes.

We headed back to the house. Seth arrived soon after. Abel, our locksmith son, was helping people get into their cars and houses and would try to reach us as soon as he could. We continued to pack the fifth wheel. The official word had been to pack a 72 hour bag. And so I did.

I did think to grab our passports (which in the confusion ended up being left in the garage!) And we grabbed my computer, an iPad, a DS and other assorted electronics. We brought three days worth of clothes.

We did not bring pictures, keepsakes, treasures. After all we were only going to be gone for three days. I believed that. Perhaps there was a sense that if we did start loading up such valuables, it would mean that the unthinkable would happen. I don't know. If we had thought we would be gone for a month or more I would have packed so differently. But we didn't know.

We were so relieved when Al and Abel both arrived. At least those of us who were left in Fort McMurray were all together. That was tremendously comforting.

Al insisted that we would not leave until our subdivision, Timberlea, evacuated.

The traffic was gridlocked and he didn't want to add unnecessarily to the congestion. At this point all traffic was being sent north to the camps and he definitely didn't want to go north. He knew they would be trying to clear the highway south and he wanted to wait as long as possible for that to happen.

Seth and Abel took the truck to try and get diesel fuel. It was totally impossible. Seth left the truck to walk home, helping people along the way with mechanical problems. Abel drove back on the sidewalk. The traffic only flowed one way. With only a quarter of a tank in the truck, we knew it would be the grace of God alone that would get us to safety.

We continued to monitor the radio and the sky, walking out to the ball park to see how close the fire looked. The streets were wall to wall cars. No one could move.

Every now and again people inched forward then sat idling, waiting for the next few inches.

Finally, the mandatory evacuation call was given for Timberlea. There were no more radio announcements. The radio station had gone off the air. Everything was very quiet.

Al hooked up the fifth wheel and at 6:45 pm we pulled out of our driveway. Seth and Abel took my car, since it had fuel and neither of theirs did.

We crawled towards Confederation Way. I didn't know how we'd get through the streets with the big rig behind us. Somehow we did.

Police officers moved the traffic along. No one paid attention to the lights. We were driving east in the westbound lane, but no one was going west. Every lane of traffic was going the same way - toward highway 63, out of Fort McMurray.

When we got to the top of the hill, officers routed all that traffic into the south bound lanes. Thank God we would not be going north!

Again I made the surreal drive across the Athabasca bridge and through the "deserted" Downtown. I can't describe how uncanny it was to see so much traffic on the road out, but not a single car in the downtown core. Both the north and southbound lanes were filled with cars going south.

The stop and go driving made us glance uneasily at the fuel gauge. It held at a quarter tank. From our house to Gregoire usually takes about 20 or 25 minutes. It took us over two hours to get to the Shell station.

Bumper to bumper, crawling along, we had plenty of time to see the frightened faces of people who had pulled over to the side of the road just outside the city limits. Columns of thick black smoke filled the air behind us, while up ahead were clear blue Alberta evening skies. One of the strangest sights was massive flocks of birds flying high above us, heading north.

Seth and Abel called in. They were going to go to Anzac to try and get a jerry can of diesel for us. Gratefully, we drove on, unsure how far we would get before we ran out of fuel. We drove until 12:30 in the morning.

Just past Mariana Lake there is a rest stop. We were 18 kilometres past empty. Al decided we'd better pull in before we ran out completely. It was a miracle we got that far. We had a quarter of a tank when we left home and pulled our 39 foot trailer for five-and-a-half hours.

Christina (public relations)

My husband ran into our garage and grabbed water buckets and old towels in case we needed to make a run through flames. Luckily, finally the traffic started moving out at a fast pace.

On the way down Abasand Hill we passed a lineup of RCMP officers who were wearing masks. We slowed down to ask one which way we could go once we got to the highway, north or south, and he said to just follow the evacuation route north.

In that moment it struck me that this man probably had a wife and kids wondering if he was safe, and I reached out the window and touched his shoulder and said, "God bless you".

So we headed north, and my husband said to me what I had dreaded but knew was coming. He would get us to his fire hall at Suncor where we would be safe and then he had to go to work.

I cried and said, I know, it's the life.

So that is what he did. We stayed at the Millenium camp that night and my husband worked all night.

When he got a couple of hours break the next morning, he came to us and said that as soon as the highway opens again to go south. He needed us to go and he would meet us later.

At first I refused and said there was no way I'd leave him, but one of the other firefighters' wives pulled me aside and said that (my husband) needed us to be safe so that he could focus and do his job. I knew she was right.

So around noon, I kissed him goodbye.

I drove through smoke down Highway 63 with my two boys and dog.

Thankfully, my sister, whose husband is also a firefighter, along with her two kids, left with us in their own vehicle. After six-and-a-half hours, we finally made it to St. Albert to my sister-in-law.

Michael (layperson)

I got in my car and left the underground parkade, pulling up towards the Prairie Loop intersection. Cars were lined up all the way in both directions, and nothing was moving.

Occasionally, someone would be able to pull through the intersection and onto Riedel St., headed towards Franklin Avenue. Once in a while, a truck would cross the intersection to go down through the road construction on the way to the Snye (River--an inlet from the Clearwater River).

One gentleman did return and wave to people that it was a plausible route. That permitted a few people to go, but that was no remedy for the hundreds of others still waiting.

All the while, peace settled upon me. I'm sure it was the Holy Spirit of God. I just sat there at the edge of the drive into my complex with my hazards on with no intention of merging into line. Sometimes a driver from Prairie Loop would stop and wave to me but I'd just put my hands up, surrendering the spot in the queue so they could continue on.

I knew that the fire was not an immediate danger; but I also knew my eternity was secure. Car after car passed by as I sat idle and waiting. I did not know for what. It was an unknowing knowing if I could call it that.

About 40 minutes later, my phone rang. My good brother in Christ, Payam was on his way back from work on site, but he was having such difficulty traveling south with all the northbound traffic. He could not help but be concerned for his fiancée whom he presumed was still downtown at her apartment across from Heritage Park.

I told him where I was waiting and that I could easily get down Prairie Loop Boulevard and down King Street to her. He told me he would make a call and find out.

Again, I waited patiently. Maybe this was why I was to wait? Maybe I felt I was to wait so I could pick her up and help my brother and sister in the Lord?

A few minutes later, the phone rang again and it was Payam. Fortunately his fiancée had already gotten a ride with another friend and they were headed northbound. We wished each other well and hung up.

Then, I suddenly felt released, like it was time to leave. I had not waited for them, but the Lord had me wait for some other reason.

Slowly the traffic moved. As I neared Franklin Avenue, I saw that the fires were now raging in Abasand again. It was wild and fearsome. It was not at all the large wall of fire I expected, but it was still violent. I wondered if this would be the last time I'd see downtown as it was.

On Facebook a friend had tagged me in a post. As a journalist she was asking if any Fort McMurray friends would be interested in a phone interview. I responded that she could call if she'd like and I left my number.

When she did call, she asked questions about the damage, and the evacuation, but most importantly, about the fear and how I felt. Although my mind was alert and heightened in awareness, I felt such incredible peace. I explained to her that my peace came from God.

She replied that faith was likely helping many people, so I took the opportunity to explain that it was not faith of any variety but a true faith in Jesus Christ which gave me peace.

I explained that it was not the strength of my faith but the person I placed my faith in that made the difference.

When we concluded our conversation, I was nearing Hardin Street and could see a helicopter dropping water on City Hall, I suppose in order to protect the infrastructure for future resettlement. Because of the bomber though, traffic was now redirected left and onto Highway 63 going north.

As I passed over the river with all the cars, it was such a surreal experience. Like something out of an apocalyptic movie. The bypass bridge from Franklin Avenue was totally empty, not a car on it. But as I rounded the bend along Memorial Drive nearing the bottom of Thickwood Boulevard, I saw a lone man on that deserted bypass road.

He was waving for someone from our traffic to give him a ride.

Instantly I thought to myself that perhaps this was a fellow who's vehicle had run out of fuel or something, or perhaps he did not have a vehicle, and I quickly pulled into the exit lane towards the bypass and on-ramp to Thickwood Boulevard.

I honked to let him know my intent and he began jogging towards me. I pulled over and he got in and thanked me. He was a fellow around 50 years of age, slightly disheveled in appearance and with a trace of hard alcohol on his breath. But I was glad to see this man.

We introduced ourselves and he thanked me again for the ride. It turned out he was on days off from his work-cycle and was Downtown drinking with friends who happened to be homeless. His employment had not stopped his desire to be friends with those who were unemployed, but sadly, it had not stopped his desire to drink to excess either.

They had seen the fire, but like me weren't worried. Unlike me, no one had texted them to warn them of the danger. Eventually, police had told them they had to leave and make their way out of town. I'm not sure where his friends went, but he began walking back towards Fort McKay where he lived, hoping he could hitchhike and get a ride.

With all the people heading north, I wondered how many had passed him. Surely there'd been some time where he was on that bridge before traffic had been redirected and someone could've picked him up. Surely there were others that saw him on the bypass.

"So, just curious. How many people would you say passed by you before I stopped to pick you up?" I said to him.

His brow furrowed in thought as he cocked his head to the side, "Oh, thousands." Judging by the never-ending line of cars before and behind me, I did not doubt it for a second.

"Why did you stop to pick me up?"

My heart warmed and I smiled as I looked ahead to the traffic jam we would soon re-enter from the bypass. "Well... Jesus Christ is my Lord and Saviour and he said that anything we do to the least of these, we've done for him... and I'd like to think that if I saw Jesus walking down the road like you were, that I'd stop and pick him up."

Instantly the man's face dropped and he began to weep as he doubled over, clutching for his heart.

I looked over, concerned. "Are you alright?"

"I'm sorry," he said, "... I'm sorry for crying..."

My right hand left the wheel and rested on his shoulder in reassurance. "No need to apologize, man. There's nothing wrong with tears; but what's wrong?"

He raised his head, looking through moist and softened eyes and said, "As I walked from downtown, I was starting to get tired. So many cars passed by me and no one stopped. I knew I still had so far to go before I got home to McKay... So I prayed, 'Lord, please help me get home... Please help me get a ride...'" He paused as if for emphasis. Then looking at me he finished saying, "... And that's when you honked your horn."

God had responded to the prayers of a man because God is good and perfect. And in this moment of revelation where my new companion understood God answered that prayer immediately, he was overwhelmed and brought to tears by the goodness of God. He recognized instantly that God does hear.

My heart was so deeply touched to be a part of God's awesome answer. To think that this man had JUST prayed when I honked my horn, and that God had answered that prayer down to the second spoke so loudly of God's absolute sovereignty and His perfect timing.

Had I evacuated earlier, this would have not happened. Had I packed up quicker this would not have occurred. Had the police not redirected us, this may have ended differently. But God was in complete and total control. A person can have complete and total trust in God for their eternal salvation as well as with this temporal life.

And God had prepared me to pick that man up. God was at work in every way.

During the course of our drive, I learned that this man humbly believed that Jesus Christ was the Son of God who died for his sins, and he tried to pray every night, and he wanted to be freed of his dependence on alcohol. He'd fallen back into drinking during the grief felt for the loss of his sister only a couple of months previously. God gave me the opportunity to sit with this man in slow-moving traffic for over four hours, encouraging him, and reminding him of the truth of God and God's love for him.

It was a wonderful time of fellowship and I pray that the Lord used it to strengthen this man in his faith for God's glory.

After dropping off the hitchhiker in Fort McKay it was about 9:30 pm and I found out Grey Wolf Lodge had been filled up. Approaching the intersection towards it, the volunteer traffic directors from the sites asked me if I wanted something closer but not so nice or farther and nice.

I chose farther and nice and ended up at Suncor's Firebag Lodge. It was GORGEOUS! Nice rooms. Shared a bathroom, but so what. It had a theatre, rec. rooms, gyms, awesome cafeteria with so much good food, and a smaller room for picking up snack and lunch materials. Very excellent place to stay.

Jonathan (firefighter novelist)

Within minutes we were re-tasked to another assignment: evacuate the Intensive Care Unit at the hospital.

Without a word we set off for the hospital along with two other Fire Department members who had been operating another ambulance.

When we arrived at the parking lot of the hospital we linked up with the ICU staff and began to load patients into whatever space we could create. There were two stretcher-bound patients which we loaded one per ambulance and then filled every bench and seat with staff and patients who could walk. My ambulance had four patients and three ICU staff on board for a total of nine personnel.

Critical cargo aboard, we received our vague direction of "go north." We made our way, trying to safely maneuver through a gridlock of manned and abandoned vehicles that clogged all lanes. The journey north was a long, slow and treacherous one as my partner and the ICU staff worked to keep the patients stable in the back.

Upon our arrival at Firebag, we finally offloaded our patients at a hanger that had been converted into a medical triage centre. All four of us fire fighters were anxious to return to the city to help.

The return drive at night was an eerie one. We arrived early in the morning and made our way back to Fire Hall I Downtown.

There, it seemed like a different city. The first thing we saw was a couple horses standing with their owners in the fire department vehicle bay and drinking water out of buckets in the smoke-filled haze. Nothing was normal.

A city bus pulled into the station, driven by one of the fire department members and a city driver who had been given permission to raid one of the local grocery stores for food, medicine and other essential supplies needed by the first responders.

All of us were running on fumes, and the food tasted amazing and the eye drops helped ease the sting that myself and others felt in their smoke assaulted eyes.

So many people were coughing from the smoke inhalation, which felt as thick inside as it was outside. Many of us felt sick to the stomach or battled pulsing headaches which only added to the exhaustion we felt from the long, hard, chaotic day.

There was still so much to do. Our next assignment was to escort a group of out-of-town firefighters to Macdonald Island which had become the staging point for all the emergency vehicles, personnel and equipment that had come in throughout the night.

There we waited for our next medical call as the last of the night became morning. My partner helped treat me as the smoke had driven me to near vomiting. With some Gravol and oxygen on board, my mind and stomach settled. What helped the most to calm my nerves though, was stopping to take a moment to pray.

The conversation helped ease my spirit along with the knowledge that my wife and unborn child had made it safely to Edmonton. Knowing that felt like enough. Whatever happened up here now, to me or to the city, I felt at peace.

David (firefighter with three sons)

We went down to MacDonald Island and got about three hours of sleep before we were back at it again the next morning.

On May 4th, I was assigned to Timberlea in a pickup truck and we had a couple of lines we hooked up to hydrants. We didn't even have a pump. We went around and looked for spot fires. We were able to put out quite a few and prevent them from getting out of control.

That night we went out to Stone Creek (north side of Timberlea) and it was pretty frustrating. That was when the wind was really picking up, the fires were getting really intense, and we were calling for resources and they weren't coming. We kept getting pushed back, and pushed back.

The fire got quite bad and we lost a lot of homes there in Stone Creek. When the resources finally came, we didn't have a real task.

I'd heard over the tactical radio that there was fire out at Saprae Creek, which I was worried about. That afternoon, I asked my captain if I could go home and rescue my dogs before my house burned down; I was told no, I was needed there in Timberlea.

So I went on Facebook and put out a plea for anyone who was in the area to go rescue our dogs.

Dee (poet)

Aaron, Chloe, and I drove in a convoy toward Loutit Road. We inched into grid-locked traffic.

I put the air conditioning on, to cool the oppressive heat, and hopefully calm O'Malley behind me in his kennel. He was panting loudly. I could hear him vomit and the truck filled with an acrid odour.

I remembered my husband mentioning that using the air conditioning required more fuel, so I turned it off and opened the windows.

Thick smoke filled the cab of the yellow FJ truck. The heat made my clothes stick to me and I regretted wearing heavy jeans and a black top, which I'd chosen thinking we may be camping somewhere that night at the side of the highway.

Chloe and I had our phones on speaker, and we talked as we inched our way to the highway. I received a few texts from friends, telling me the fire was circling Timberlea.

My husband Jeff phoned and said to head north to his job site, and he would get rooms for us in the camp.

Highway 63 south was closed; we wouldn't be driving to Edmonton that night, and with most of the traffic trying to head to the highway for a southern escape, I thought our flight north would be quicker.

But with over a third of the near 90,000 residents living in Timberlea, plus Thickwood residents crawling around Confederation Way through Timberlea, it seemed impossible. The roads were clogged with vehicles so RCMP vehicles drove on sidewalks and meridians.

Water bombers roared past randomly, giant sky-tankers dropping water and fire retardant.

An occasional helicopter added to the pandemonium. At intersections, people disregarded the lights and alternated. Traffic lightened a little as we made it north into Parson's Creek. We saw people barbecuing and sitting in lawn chairs.

I called out, "Mandatory evacuation... everyone has to leave!"

My sister texted to say I should head north to a work camp. Our convoy crawled north to Parson's Creek overpass highway access, just in time to be directed south by an RCMP officer; south through the flames, south to Edmonton. What a relief. What a terror.

Chloe said a friend of hers had jumped the meridian in her little car, outrunning police, racing through the flames, just as the police were closing the southern route. Would it be any safer now?

Traffic was a little faster moving on the highway, but only until we reached Downtown. Aaron was able to shoot ahead so we lost him to the onward crowd. Trees blazed with hot-orange flames on the right side of the road covering the north side of Abasand Hill.

"We have to drive through the flames. I don't know if I can do it," Chloe said.

"Stay right on my bumper," I told her. "Look straight ahead at my truck. Don't look at the fire." Heavy smoke impaired our visibility. Flames wildly licked tree trunks and shot up from the scorched grass at the base of Abasand Hill as we passed along its east side.

"Oh my goodness... look at all the damage," I said.

"Just look ahead," she reminded me. I could barely see the car in front, but then the smoke thinned.

"I can't believe it," I said. Sideways glances gave me glimpses of firefighters working, hosing down flames on both sides of the highway.

"Keep going... don't look at the fire," Chloe said. A single house on Crescent Heights burning, a lone fire fighter with an ax, working to put it out; the backyard fence gone, the roof of the house collapsed, the yard scarred with black. They'd stopped it from going into Downtown, I thought.

Onward south, we drove up, out of the river valley with Waterways and Draper to the left of us, Beacon Hill to the right.

"Oh my gosh! Oh my gosh! Oh my gosh! There's no Waterways left!" and a few minutes later, "Beacon Hill! No houses in Beacon Hill!" I said. A berm partially blocked the view, but normally houses were visible.

Abandoned vehicles were stuck in the ditches. A commuter bus, door open, was empty and stuck in the low gulch. It was like a scene from Left Behind.

Vehicles travelled south; but first responders travelled north towards the fire. RCMP motioned to traffic with both arms, directing south-- go on both sides of the divided highway--go south.

Once out of the city, more and more vehicles were pulled over at the side of the highway. Some were resting, some feeding babies. Children played among the vehicles, adults having a drink. Others looked like they were out of gas, and people loaded with gas and water were coming to their aid.

Alarmed by the email I'd sent them, family continued to text throughout the night, checking on our progress. My friend Ellie texted from Fort Saskatchewan wondering if we needed gas: people were on their way north with supplies.

We stopped finally, too. I pulled out of the never-ending line of cars and trucks and put on my emergency flashers. I crossed down into the ditch, soaking one leg up to the knee in mud.

I climbed out and went on to the shelter of trees and brush in search of privacy. As I came back out, I took a moment to look at the city aflame. Massive billows of smoke, moisture, ash.

Exhausted, I got back in the truck. I didn't know how long it would take to get to Edmonton, but we had to press on. Surely the traffic should lighten at some point.

At 2 am, Chloe and I were exhausted. Aaron had texted. He was much further ahead. He told us his girlfriend was camping at the side of the highway north, near Suncor, with her parents, but they planned to meet in Edmonton.

I was concerned about my fuel level. I had a quarter tank of gas when we passed a line-up at Wandering River. We continued past Grassland as well, hoping for shorter lines at the next stop.

We decided to pull over and try to sleep at the side of the road. O'Malley and his kennel reeked horribly. I took him out of his kennel and he was nervous with all the bumper-to-bumper traffic (still), and excited about being outside for a walk.

I offered to walk the puppy while Chloe rinsed out the kennel and wiped it with paper towel. Afterwards, we decide to bunk together in the yellow truck. We set up pillows and sleeping bags with reclined seats.

We prayed together for everyone and tried to sleep, but the dull roar of persistent traffic coupled with our frayed nerves and exhaustion wouldn't allow it. Finally, we decided to merge back into traffic and continue on.

A while later, we rolled into Boyle as the sun was coming up. A young woman was yelling at her husband in the cab of their truck, saying she was tired and hungry. He was trying to calm her down.

 She yelled and shrieked and cried. She was obviously overcome from the harrowing escape. It was frightening to hear their exchange.

I had berated myself for my anxiousness at times, but apparently God had given us his peace nonetheless, which was obvious in comparison to their anguish.

I scrambled to gather some food for the young woman, planning to take her apples and granola bars, but before I could, the husband gunned the gas pedal and they roared away. All I could do was pray for them.

It took us all night, but we finally reached Edmonton 12 hours after leaving home.

JD (radio announcer & reporter)

Finally, we got to my house in Timberlea, on Eglert Drive. I was able to get my laptop, my Bible, some clothes, my birth certificate, and passport. That was it.

Everything else was just stuff, but there were memories. That was something I really battled with over the next weeks until we found out the house was okay for which I thank God.

We went to my boss's house where she gathered a few things. Her daughter and their dog joined us in the car. We left Timberlea at about 5:30 pm to head for the highway.

It took about three and a half hours, as we were moving very slowly. Some people got out of their cars and peed at the side of the road. Some people were wandering around, not aware of how serious the situation was. We offered many people rides.

Around 11 pm, we stopped between Suncor and Fort McKay at a roadside turnout. My boss and her daughter leaned their seats back and slept. I dozed off for maybe a total of 45 minutes and then the dog would lick my face. In between, I was on Twitter. At 5:45 the next morning, I had the first of about 45 interviews across Canada in radio, print media, and TV.

I found out my friend Alix and the team at Dunvegan Gardens had to drive through the fire to get out. Theirs wasn't an easy way out, but God was faithful and provided a way. It was remarkable.

Wednesday May 4th, we made our way to Fort McKay with about a quarter tank of gas. After waiting in line for about half an hour, we realized we weren't going to get gas. At that point, we decided to leave it in God's hands. We weren't certain how far we'd get. We saw abandoned vehicles everywhere. I wasn't certain if I'd ever get home--to my home in Central Alberta.

We headed south, through Fort McMurray. As we neared the top of Supertest Hill, our vehicle filled up with smoke from the fire, and it was worse as we neared the city. I smelled like a campfire and I hadn't left the vehicle.

I shot some video as we drove through. We took the bypass lane to drive along the highway. I saw the charred remains of Abasand Hill. We continued south on the highway, and we saw the Super 8 Hotel and Denny's still on fire. We saw hundreds of abandoned vehicles. It looked like the Apocalypse; like a scene out of the Walking Dead where you expect zombies to jump out. It was grim. It was unbearable.

I was confident throughout the time that God was in control, but my faith was surely tested as I wasn't sure if I was getting out of it alive or not. When my sister prayed I received peace that I'd never experienced before which I can't even describe, but absolutely, my faith was tested.

Again, literally hundreds of vehicles were abandoned. Others were driving and exiting the city, for what we thought could very well be the last time. The fire continued to burn and we didn't know if we would have a city to return to. I felt deeply thankful to all of the first responders who were willing to face the Beast, to stare it in the face. There are no words to describe how indebted I am to the first responders.

Some of my friends stayed behind and breathed in smoke and soot for days. I thank God for protecting them.

We had little more than 20 kilometres worth of gas when we reached a mobile fuel unit on Highway 63 south. It was over 30 degrees C, and someone came and gave us each a bottle of cold water. What a treat. After about 45 minutes of waiting, we thought we would receive just enough gas to make it to Edmonton, perhaps a quarter tank. But the person filled up the tank completely. We cried. At that point we would have paid a million dollars for gas.

We just wanted to get away from the fire; we just wanted to be with our loved ones in Central Alberta. So, thank you to the heroes who gave us gas without expecting anything in return.

Late in the day, we arrived in Athabasca. The Teen burger I had at A&W was the best thing I had ever tasted. It had been about 44 hours since I'd last eaten.

At 8:30 Wednesday evening, I arrived home to my family near Rocky Mountain House. My family was all ready and waiting for me there. And they all cheered me on as I came into the house. And the incredible hugs from my family were a beautiful thing as I hadn't known that I would ever see them again.

Elizabeth (artist)

Police officers were directing traffic. I was texting periodically when stopped, to keep in touch with my sister notifying her about the fire situation, telling her she and her family needed to leave right away. I was trying to decide if I should meet up with her or head out of town south or go north, on my own. My sister told me to pick up her husband if I went north. He was not being bused home from work. I was trying to decide what the safest way to go would be, still being able to see the massive smoke bellowing up from Thickwood Heights in front of me.

When I reach the intersection of Paquette Drive and Confederation Way, a police officer directed me to turn around and go to the new overpass heading north. I didn't want to head north; the decision was made for me. I had been heading to join up with my sister and her family. She said her hubby told her to get the kids and pets and head south out of town.

Now I had to go north and didn't know where the new over pass was. I decided to follow the car in front of me. I prayed to the Lord to help me to know where to go. I followed the other cars until I came to a fork by the new overpass and had to decide to go south or go north.

I pulled over and thought about it and also asked the police at the fork of the road, what was going on. They said I could go south if I wanted to because the highway was open right then.

I looked at my gas tank and there was not enough gas to make it to the gas station at Wandering River. Then I looked at the huge cloud of smoke. I made a quick decision to go north.

I saw bumper-to-bumper traffic: cars, vans, campers and many different vehicles stopping along the way. I thought I am not sure what to do now. I still had the radio on and heard that if you were before the Suncor underpass, they had rooms available for whoever needed a place to sleep. Just seconds before, I would have driven under the Suncor overpass.

With only seconds to spare, I made a sharp right turn just in time to make the turn off to get a room at Suncor camp. I thought, 'Thank you Lord!' God is never early, or late, He is always right on time.

Alisa (engineer)

As it turned out, regular people would help us. I didn't see one single firefighter on May 3rd. That day, those that I remember working their jobs to perfection, to keep order and thus keep us safe, were teachers, DJs, and police officers.

When I pulled out of the grocery store, I instinctively turned on the radio. The DJ on 100.5 was calm but gave quick, detailed updates. All of the schools were being evacuated. I had to decide which of my kids to pick up first.

At 2:15 pm, I strode across the playground of St. Anne's elementary school and collected my daughter in her classroom. Her teacher was calm, but behind in the class some kids were crying.

I passed a friend in the hallway who told me that the roads to Father Mercredi High School were "still moving well".

We still had to sign out. The staff at St. Anne's was impressive. Half a dozen teachers were gathered at the front door with clipboards, and they signed us out quickly.

As we drove towards Father Mercredi High School, I dreaded what would await us there. There were about 1,500 students in my son's school and on a normal day, the drop-off traffic backed-up onto Thickwood Boulevard.

We pulled right into the bus circle at the school. I was amazed. It was busy, but orderly. The principal and vice principal were both out on the front sidewalk. Natasha, the Principal, was talking on a cell phone and she looked worried. Brendon, the Vice Principal, told us to go "straight to the office."

We walked quickly through the front atrium. There was a short line up of parents. We moved up to the administrative assistant. I don't even know her name, but the image of her standing behind her desk, paging students to the office will never leave me.

She had the PA microphone in her hand, and called names so fast I could not see her breathe. She didn't ask twice and she didn't get any wrong. My son was suddenly behind me in the office and we were back in the van within minutes.

Now with both kids in the car and heading back home, there was time to process what was happening.

I kept the radio tuned in. Soon we heard the three emergency horns.

My daughter told me later my face changed when I heard that horn. I know my stomach tightened.

To me, this was a sound normally reserved for disaster movies, not one you expected to hear in your own car, in your own city.

The Director of Operations at the radio station now addressed us.

We learned that our own neighbourhood was not yet under evacuation. I told the kids our plan. We would unpack our groceries, load the car, and wait for John to get home from work.

When we got home, that plan was already a bust.

My husband called and said he wasn't able to get home from site. We decided instead to convoy with a good friend who lived just two blocks away.

We loaded our dog into the van and left.

We spent the next three hours sitting in unimaginable gridlock. We only moved a few blocks from our street out onto the main boulevard, Confederation Way.

There, we sat bumper to bumper, six lanes wide, everyone trying to head to the highway. Ash was falling on our cars.

We could see flames way behind us, over rooftops. We switched to the country music station, 93.3, when the others went off the air. We listened to the DJs tell us calmly what was happening with our city.

There were no firefighters or water bombers where we were. The scene unfolding around us was surreal. On our right-hand side, dirt bikes and ATVs were passing us on the sidewalk. Trucks tried to join them too, but were stopped by Bylaw. At one point, on the left side, a girl passed by on horseback.

We were in a full stop across from the police and fire station when Country 93.3 also went off the air. We had been listening to two DJs, one of whom was Taylor Pope, my son's soccer coach.

The information was the only official word we got that day. They told us what direction to drive, what camps were open, and their voices were reassuring. I remember the lonely feeling I got when they told us, "Ok folks, the RCMP are here, we are being told we have to go."

It was maybe about 5 or 6 o'clock when we saw the first police officer. I almost cried when I saw him. He was on foot, patrolling the Confederation median. He stopped at car windows, answered people's questions and kept people calm by his presence.

The whole trip, I only recall seeing a few officers.

Shortly after that, some bulldozers that had been blocking the lanes turned off, and traffic started moving. We finally eased into the first intersection controlled by RCMP.

And minutes after that, we were riding towards the highway ramp. There, an officer directed us to turn north onto Highway 63. I gave her thumbs up as I blinked back tears of relief.

We crawled along for another few hours to get to site. We felt safer under the blue sky, away from the smoke, but it was still tiring. There were cars and campers and RVs as far as the eye could see.

Vehicles were parked two-thick along both sides of the road. Many had run out of gas, many more were camping for the night.

One guy was sitting in the back of his pickup playing guitar.

When we arrived at the Syncrude gate at about 9:30 pm, I was exhausted.

David (firefighter with three sons)

So one of the other firefighters who was on light duty, Chris, a good friend of mine now, saw my plea for help on Facebook and drove out to Saprae Creek with one of the squads, and got two of my dogs. Our rescue dog, Riley, was skittish and hid, and Chris couldn't get him to come, so had to leave him there. They took my dogs to stay in one of the fire hall boardrooms, which is where they stayed for a week.

In the meantime, my wife, Jen, who had been evacuated north, was later sent south to Edmonton. Michelle, our neighbour, evacuated south with our kids, and my wife rendezvoused with her and was able to get our kids. My family took a flight to Ottawa early on May 4th, to stay with family.

About midnight, we were able to take a pickup truck and drive out to my place to check the status. I was thinking my third dog, Riley, was a goner.

All my wood piles were on fire. And it was catching on to my friend Aaron's sailboat, and my friend Hans's camper. My truck and camper were next to that, and my siding was catching fire.

The boys with me grabbed a hose, but there was no water supply. If we could have put out the fire on the siding, we could have saved the house.

I went into the house, and there was Riley, looking at me like, "Hey dad, what's going on?" I grabbed him and threw him into the pickup truck.

I was able to go around and grab some important things, like the laptop with photos and a few other things that were important to us.

I phoned my wife in Ottawa. It was 2 am. She answered the phone groggily.

I said, "Hey Hon, our house is burning down, what do you want me to save?"

She said to get the kids' blankies, the dogs' medicine, dog food. I packed a quick bag of clothes, my Bible, my rifle, a couple other things, and that's it.

The guys said, "Hey, do you want to save your pickup truck?"

But because of the work we'd been doing in the yard, I hadn't secured the camper back onto the truck. I didn't want it to come off on the road, so I left it. Unfortunately it all burned.

Jonathan (firefighter novelist)

I knew that the first battle was done, but I also knew that the war was far from over. From that point forward we turned the medical response over to AHS and my partner and I were moved to firefighting tasks.

I took various positions, from leading a group of out-of-town firefighters in the defence of Downtown, to battling against the seemingly out of control inferno in Stone Creek (Timberlea).

I also dedicated time to help slow the fire's advance in Abasand and finally, in assisting the ongoing efforts of extinguishing hot spots that constantly flared up throughout the city.

This was my life for the majority of that week: patrolling through fire ravaged areas, watching for the smallest sign of smoke or flame and then, when discovered, attacking the flare-ups while they were small, to avoid their spreading.

While driving through many areas, things appeared peaceful and still, until at any time, a strong gust of wind would literally push flames up from underneath the surface of the earth and towards unburned fences, yards, trees and homes.

Oftentimes we had only minutes to react and contain the fire. The work was constant, hard and intensified by the hot, smoke-filled conditions.

For me, one of the most powerful images of the fire was from my time in Stone Creek. When we were dispatched there, we were advised to "turn onto Prospect (Drive) and follow the smoke". When the entire sky is filled with smoke it hit me just how intensely that fire was raging.

Enormous billowing clouds of thick black smoke rose up into the setting sun of the evening sky to the north.

The smoke obscured everything, making it hard to find another pumper truck or any of my fellow fire fighters.

When we finally pushed through the smoke and arrived on scene, I witnessed a sight I will never forget. The thick black smoke gave way to its relentless source. Both sides of the city street ahead of me were roaring powerfully, entirely consumed by flames.

Houses, cars, fences, trees, grass, everything was on fire.

It all blended together in a brilliant whirlwind of roaring flames that only vaguely revealed the shapes of what was burning.

The intense flames and thick black smoke obscured the sight of anything beyond that immediate street.

The sound was unforgettable. A howling fire storm, accompanied by alarms beeping from vehicles, fully consumed in flames.

A steady stream of explosions boomed across the sky as propane and fuel tanks exploded. Glass was shattering everywhere, and the crack of collapsing houses punctuated it all.

With so much on fire and being this close to it, the heat waves ran over us, pushing us back as powerful winds hurled toxic smoke at us.

We squinted our eyes and tried to cover our faces with whatever we had, but our efforts did little. It was like looking at Hell itself. All we could do was fight, so we did.

Thomas (father to seven children)

Nobody honked. Nobody road raged. And most importantly, nobody panicked. We were all headed for the community of Anzac, a reputed safe refuge for any and all fleeing the inferno that was ravenously consuming Fort McMurray.

The lineup of cars, trucks, buses, and RVs snaked towards the hamlet carefully, almost gingerly, respecting each other and our common desire to find somewhere, anywhere, safe.

Just before Anzac is a little white church atop a small hill, gracefully cradled by trees. It looked like the type of refuge I needed. I turned into the lot, not wanting to carry on in the long line up of cars and trucks. As we pulled up the long gravel driveway, I noticed that the church door was open. I hoped that was a good sign.

As I pulled around to the side of the building, a figure appeared in the doorway, paused for a moment, then started walking purposefully toward us.

He was a young looking pastor, light-haired with a friendly smile and a calm voice. Before I even asked the question, he reassured me that we were welcome, for as long as we needed to stay, and would provide whatever they had if it would help.

"I'd appreciate if we could park the trailer and stay the night. And if you have some water for the kids that would be awesome." I couldn't bring myself to explain that I was missing four of my group of seven at the moment.

During the long, slow drive I had been texting the babysitter and new found hero to find out the status of my kids, whether she had picked them up, where they were headed, and if they were all safe. Communication networks were overloaded, if not burned up, so it was a slow, anxious process. No answer yet.

"There's water in the church, as much as you need. And you can park the trailer around back if you like." the pastor was explaining.

I nodded numbly, put Vincent into gear and pulled the trailer to the indicated area. The procedure of setting up and leveling the trailer was a welcome distraction for a few moments. I needed that. I took my kids with me into the church for bathroom breaks and water. There was a small play room for the kids as we entered, and they immediately made for it. A welcome reprieve for three bewildered babies. As I watched them play, the pastor reappeared.

"Can I pray with you?" he asked gently.

"Yeah, I'd appreciate that," I responded quietly, and then added, "I'm missing four of my kids. They're somewhere with a stranger, leaving Fort McMurray."

I was beginning to resolve that no tears would flow from my eyes for the unknown, but they threatened to cloud my vision anyway. My heart ached. I took a deep breath as the pastor absorbed what I had just said, his expression showing understanding and grace.

I don't remember what he prayed, but I do remember feeling stronger. I would get through this, I would have ALL of my kids back, and somehow, someday, somewhere, this would all just be an unpleasant memory.

I settled the kids into their beds some time later that night, using jackets as pillows, with a few blankets I'd managed to grab covering their tired little bodies, tucking in arms and legs as best I could. Darkness was settling in, and I walked outside to look to the north. Red and orange clouds of smoke and fire were all I could see. It was all anyone could see, as the church's lot had turned into a refuge for dozens of people. We all stared in silent shock as it sunk in that at this very moment our homes could be consumed by this beast of a fire. It was too much.

I couldn't keep watching, or thinking about what we were escaping, so I went back inside. My five-year-old, Zach met me at the door, the other two having fallen asleep some time earlier.

"What's up, Buster?" I asked as gently as I could.

"Are Allie, and Tories, and Nick, and Ben okay?" he asked in his usual quiet, careful voice.

It took me a moment to take a deep, calming breath before I could talk.

"I'm really not sure, my boy, but I think so." I hoped so, I prayed so, I wanted desperately so. But at the moment there was absolutely nothing I could do. I'd made my way to the couch, maneuvering quietly and carefully so I didn't wake anyone.

Zach joined me there, quickly crawled onto my lap, rested his head on my chest and sighed. "I really hope so, Daddy."

I couldn't speak, or maybe wouldn't for fear of losing it completely.

I don't know how long we sat there, a Dad comforting his son missing four siblings, and a son giving his dad something to focus on, keeping the three kids he did have safe. The sound of a text coming through on my phone broke the silence.

"We drove through the fire and are on our way to Anzac. Where are you?" It was the babysitter! I quickly informed her of where we were, hoping it would go through quickly. It did! Now all we had to do was wait. My boy Zach was still sitting on my lap.

"Is everything okay, Daddy?" he asked sleepily.

"I'm thinking it might be, son," I replied with refreshed hope. It was something to hang on to.

I don't know how long me and my boy waited in the dark, silently and anxiously awaiting more of my children, more of his brothers and sister. It seemed like an eternity. I still didn't know where my oldest was, either, but I would have three more.

It was late, somewhere around midnight I think, when I heard a truck pulling up close to the church. With all the other traffic driving by I'm not sure how, but I knew my kids were in that truck.

As I've now taken to calling her, Naomi the Hero was out of the truck first. I was very tempted to hug her, but didn't know if I'd be able to keep it together, or whether I'd let her go again, or how I would ever thank her enough for rescuing three of my children.

Instead, in the faint light coming from the windows of the church, all I could muster for the moment was a "Thank you so much." I wanted to say so much more, but couldn't. Those damn tears were threatening me again, and I still had one child I had to find. Not yet, I told myself. There might be time later.

Cheerfully she responded with, "No problem, I'm glad I could help!"

No problem waiting for almost three hours at a school surrounded by fire, trying to find kids you've never met before, calming and caring for them as you painstakingly drove through a city on fire with thousands of other people, to get to their almost insane father almost ten hours later. She needs a cape, I thought.

Three of my kids appeared from the truck, and we hugged, tightly, for a long time. I thanked Naomi again, found that she'd be staying in Anzac for the night with friends, then she got back into her truck and drove off.

Stories about lava, and fire, and smoke, and being scared, and Naomi was so nice poured excitedly out of the mouths of these three of my group of seven. We walked towards the trailer, all of us holding hands with each other, tightly.

An hour or so later, I finally had the new batch of kids tucked in wherever and with whatever I could find to keep them warm, or at least somewhat comfortable.

As I was about to settle into my bed for the night, shutting off remaining lights on the way and making sure the trailer door was locked, my boy Zach suddenly appeared beside me again.

"It's really, really, super late, my boy," I said. "It's time for bed. Are you okay?"

I could see he really wanted to say something. Sometimes, with this one, it took patience to coax whatever thoughts he was having out. I knelt down to his level and waited. This was going to be deep for my boy.

He frowned slightly as he began to speak. "Okay... and Daddy?" Zach said, as he moved in to squeeze my neck with his little boy arms, gentle tears forming in his dark brown eyes, "Thanks for keeping us safe, Daddy." It was all he could muster.

And I'm not sure I would've been able to handle much more. Simple, powerful, heart shaking words. I couldn't breathe as I pulled my son in close for a warm, soul connecting hug before sending him back to bed.

"I love you, boy. And that's all I can do." As hard as I tried, I couldn't keep a few tears from falling as I let him go back to bed. I only had one more of my group of seven to find, and I was hoping it would be soon.

The night in Anzac was restless. Aside from the perpetual stream of survivors pulling in to find refuge, I was also up constantly, making sure none of my six children had somehow disappeared. I was a male mother hen, fretting about every little sound, checking the window outside to see if the fire was creeping any closer, and wondering where my oldest daughter was; my Allie-boo. She's smart, and tough I thought to myself.

I wrestled with the urge to start driving again or stay put, or anything to pass the time while the fire was causing whatever as of yet unknown devastation to our home. Our lives were suddenly upside down. I didn't have my lovely wife by my side, we had little food, but we did have water. With water, we can survive, I thought. At least that's what TV shows said.

I wondered where the water was to fight the fire, why we'd had such little warning. And why had we all been thrown into it such a huge atrocity. And finally, before I fell into sleep, I wondered why this had to happen when I had finally convinced my wife to take a trip of her own after years of taking care of our little ones.

I woke just as I had fallen asleep. Restless, unsure, and desperately trying to figure out what to do next.

The answer came in a text from my Allie. She was in Wandering River! They had driven through and out of the inferno. My heart leapt as I read the words, the realization of her safety almost dropping me to my knees. Those damn tears were threatening my eyes again, promising to overwhelm me if I let them. I couldn't. I wouldn't. Not yet. There was still one to gather.

We were packed up in no time and everybody was in Vincent the van. I started the engine, scanning gauges. Everything looked good except the fuel level. Without pulling the trailer it would have been no problem to get to Wandering River and points south before having to refuel, but we were pulling that monstrosity (thankfully), and I had to get to my daughter. I weighed the odds of waiting it out in Anzac, or heading south. Sometimes the heart is an amazingly powerful member in the decision making process. My Allie was south. I did another quick head count, then put the van in gear.

It seemed we were going the wrong way, as there was an incredibly long line-up heading the exact opposite way. I briefly wondered if I was making the right choice, banished any thought otherwise and continued, every second getting closer to making my family whole again.

We came to the intersection of Highway 63 and the turnoff to Anzac. I looked to the north and was stunned by the absolutely massive cloud of angry fire smoke obliterating any promise of blue sky. It crept, no surged upwards, and it looked like it wanted more. More houses, more cities, more fire. I don't know if there's any way to describe the anger I felt at that moment; an anger bordering on rage. I wanted to scream, "How dare you threaten my family! Everyone's families!? What have we done to have this?!" And then I glanced south and thought, not today you don't. I'm going to get the last one, and you won't be able to touch her! I turned south, not even looking in my mirrors to give that damn fire the satisfaction.

I drove carefully, not pushing the van too hard in an effort to conserve fuel. The fuel gauge was dropping too fast. We weren't going to make it, but we had to keep going. Half tank, then a while later creeping up on a quarter. Where were the telltale curves in the road to tell me Wandering River was close? Under a quarter, pushing into the red. How am I going to get six of my kids to safety in this blistering heat? I reminded myself we still had water, and we could walk if we had to.

Deep into the red now, almost at the "E" mark. Then they were there. The curves! And on those curves were parked at least a hundred vehicles, all waiting to get fuel, supplies, whatever they could from the oasis of the north known as Wandering River. The fuel gauge was on "E", but at least we were close. I wondered how long before the van would sputter and stall, gasping the last vapours of gas.

We were in that line up for almost three hours, and it didn't. That wonderful, faithful van didn't stall, didn't sputter, didn't even hint at giving up. As we finally pulled up to the pump for our turn, those ever present tears threatened me again. As I made everyone promise to stay in the van while I fuelled, I patted the dash of the van, thanking whoever made it so reliable. Another miracle despite The Beast. Or perhaps in spite of it.

With all the busyness in Wandering River, I decided texting Allie would be the best way to find out where she was. No reply. I waited. Nothing. Had they gone further south? Had they run out of phone battery? Were they in trouble? Whirling thoughts, trying to scare me into panic. I decided we had to keep moving south.

"Daddy, we're heading to Boyle! The phone ran out of battery, so I'm sorry for not texting sooner, but that's where we're going." Allie texted. I knew where I was going, then. I had a mission to accomplish, and I was getting closer to completion.

We met up with Allie at the Husky gas station in Boyle. Tired, sweaty, and smelling of smoke, but I had my Allie! I talked briefly with the lady that had driven through the fire to get out of Fort McMurray, finding out that she had lost her house, as did many of her relatives. Too shocked to feel emotion, she nodded numbly as I empathized with her. I thanked her sincerely for taking care of my daughter, and we parted ways. We both had missions to accomplish.

Joe (RCMP & Harley rider)

Shortly after arriving at our office in Timberlea, we were evacuating the building to set up post at the South Policing Facility. The air quality in Timberlea had become extremely poor. I worked alongside the Operations Officer from Wood Buffalo Detachment; a lot had to happen in a very short period of time. Extra resources would be arriving, coordinating duties and other necessities needed to begin taking shape in short order.

I didn't get to see a lot of the community in the early stages of my time in Fort McMurray; we worked all night and well into the morning. We managed to secure accommodations at a camp north of town. The Operations Officer and myself, likely managed a couple of hours of sleep before getting a call that the Emergency Operations Centre was being evacuated and we had to make our way to meet up with our dayshift colleagues near Anzac. The fun part was that the road through the city had become impassable due to fire and smoke. After arranging a change-out of front line members from our end, we were flown by helicopter to meet up with the dayshift command team.

Now dark, the City of Fort McMurray looked like a war zone with fires spread throughout. In the distance of the vast forest surrounding Fort McMurray, fires were literally everywhere. I remember as we ended up on the south side of the city above Highway 63, the fire to the east was a straight line across, a wall moving south towards Gregoire Lake and Anzac; it seemed to be as far east as the eye could see.

Once we met up with the dayshift command team, our objective was to re-establish command at the Emergency Operations Centre in the City. I know the Operations Officer and the other Staff Sergeant who were with us were a little uncomfortable when we tried to get back into the city. The fire was on both sides of the highway near the gun range and visibility about from the windshield to the front of the vehicle, but we moved along into the city regardless.

I remember, as I drove, I looked over at the Operations Officer and noticed he was leaning forward in the seat. I imagine he was trying to see further ahead and I laughed at him and pointed out that I really didn't think leaning forward was going to give him that much of an advantage.

The fire seemed to chase Emergency Operations around for the first two days, and as chaotic as it was, in a very short time we managed to establish a flow to the work at hand. I didn't spend much, if any time outside of the Emergency Operations Centre.

On Friday morning, after working long hours and getting about five or six hours sleep since arriving on Tuesday, some of us were sent home to have a break. I drove back home for the weekend and had to return on May 9th.

PART V

DISPLACED

Christina (public relations)

We stayed in St. Albert for four days and then headed further south to Okotoks because I knew if my husband got to fly out he would be sent to Calgary.

We waited in a hotel room for three more days and finally he joined us. He knew when he saw us that I needed to get into a better situation before he had to go back to work in a few days.

I guess I looked tired from watching the two boys, dog, oh and being five months pregnant stuck in a hotel. We packed up the few things we had and headed to Cape Breton so I could have the support of family.

He's been commuting every seven days.

Danelle (work-at-home mom)

There wasn't much sleep that night. We got word from responders in Fort McMurray that our house was miraculously still standing. It was a relief to hear, but we tried to stay realistic about hot spots and flare ups. The house could still go.

Early Wednesday morning, I heard the highway had opened again to southbound traffic. Drew confirmed the house was still there on his way through and began the trek south. It took him all day, but we were finally reunited on Wednesday. It was such a relief to be back together.

The following weeks were humbling and inspiring but also held many trials and were a roller coaster of emotions.

The way Alberta and Canada came together to support Fort McMurray will forever be a testament to what it means to truly be Canadian. We kept saying that people had to stop being so generous and nice to us because that's what made us cry.

Wina (backcountry enthusiast)

This has been quite an emotional week as our family along with ALL of Fort McMurray were evacuated from our city. The kindness that has been shown us by the extremely generous, thoughtful people of Edmonton is just overwhelming.

A couple of weeks ago, Kelsey (my daughter) ordered flowers for me to be delivered for Mother's Day. Well, that wasn't going to happen now.

Yesterday we all spent the day getting organized at the Evacuation Centre, then we parted our ways for the day. She is staying with friends, we are at a campground in Spruce Grove.

Kelsey then called me to say she wanted to see me, so I told her I'd grab some KFC and we'd sit down and relax at our campsite. Little did I know what she did. She called a florist at All About Flowers, to see if they had anything left. Mother's Day Is the biggest day of the year (for florists), and in Fort McMurray, if you don't order early, you don't get.

She told the florist that she had paid for her flowers in Fort McMurray but we are no longer there. And with everything that was happening she wanted "something to feel normal for her mom".

The florist asked her what her mother likes and she said my dad usually buys her two dozen red roses. Kelsey was having a hard time talking through her tears.

The florist said "Come over in an hour." She did. She walked through (the flower shop) door, and the florist said, "Are you Kelsey?"

Kelsey broke down crying.

The florist said, "This is on us."

God bless my precious daughter; I love you Kelsey. God bless the people of Edmonton. God bless you at All About Flowers. You touched all our hearts to the core. You gave us that special "Mother's Day Moment" that helped us forget our trials for a time.

Diane (active living devotee)

I'm not sure my son will ever fully realize how his cool head and calm voice helped me stay focused. He is an amazing young man.

My husband met up with us about a half hour later. He and a co-worker had managed to leave work at the (oil sands) plants. My husband had been a similar lifeline to the wife of that co-worker who was also trying to escape Beacon Hill with their young son.

Initially, we felt blessed to be alive. We assumed our home was gone. The next day, we discovered that our home had been spared despite the firefighters being pulled out of our subdivision.

When we looked at the aerial footage of the fire, it was a miracle that anything in Beacon Hill was still standing. We were in awe. There was no logical explanation for it. We were amazed that the whole town evacuated and almost 90,000 people escaped. We thanked God that the highway had been twinned as people would have been trapped otherwise. We wondered if the major impetus behind the twinning of the highway (the death of a pastor, his family and friends) was all part of God's plan to save so many people later. I can't see how it wasn't.

God showed up again when it became obvious we needed a different place to stay. We were very blessed to have friends take us while we were on evacuation. What was supposed to be a short term stay resulted in a two month intermingling of our families and lives. They listened when we needed it. They gave us space when we needed it. Their children provided a welcome distraction with innocence that only children can provide.

Instead of being the ones to open our doors, we were humbled to be on the receiving end of such a gift. It is one for which we will be eternally grateful.

Then there was the angel encounter. The Bible tells us that angels live amongst us and I believe that with all my heart. I often wondered if I would recognize an angel encounter if I was in that situation. During the evacuation, I took my daughter out to Ontario to visit my parents and sister.

My niece, my daughter and I went to Niagara Falls for the day as a special trip. We got lost getting back out to the highway and in the process of turning around in a parking lot, a guy on a bicycle collided with my car and flew over the hood. An ambulance was called, I was freaking out, and the RCMP showed up.

As I was crying, a lady came over and put her hand on my arm. She urged me to pray and reminded me that God would take of it. It brought me up short. I was so busy worrying about the man and what would happen if I was charged that

I hadn't thought to pray. I took a moment and asked for God's help in the situation. Long story short, the biker was fine, the RCMP did not lay any charges and I was free to go.

I looked for the lady to thank her, but she was gone. I have no doubt that she was an angel sent to minister in a time of need.

David (firefighter with three sons)

We went back to the boardroom and I laid out a mat on the floor with the dogs and caught a couple hours of sleep. Every day, I'd go back and let the dogs out to pee and eat, and back they'd go. It was like staying in a kennel for them.

On the third day, I went back to Saprae to confirm that our house had burned down. There was just a hole of the basement. It was surreal. I wasn't too upset, but it was a blow. It was all going to be dust and ashes one day anyway. What was important was that my family got out; my wife and kids, and dogs were safe. I got the important things like pictures. But the rest of it was just stuff that burned. All replaceable.

That was the general thought (among the fire fighters); most of the guys (firefighters) were alright. Some were pretty shaken up, but the general thought was that it was just stuff. Out of 90,000 people, only two perished, so that was huge.

When you look back over the photos and video, for all the panic and people in Beacon Hill with direct flame impingement on their vehicles, no one got trapped, or burned, or killed. It's phenomenal. It's definitely a God thing. All the credit goes to the Lord for that.

I spent most of the rest of the time out in Saprae Creek helping out with the volunteer fire department out there. I got clearance to do that. I felt it would be appropriate to support the community I live in directly.

One of my former renters came up and said he had fire experience, so he came up (from out of town), and helped out. It was incredible to bond with the local guys in Saprae, and fight shoulder to shoulder with them. We fought mostly hotspots, ground fires, and muskeg fire. It was good experience. Lots of hard work.

Following the initial days, I worked for a solid week. I got cleared on Sunday to go back on shift, to a six-days-on, six-days-off shift. I stayed in Saprae for three of those (first days off). Then I went down to Edmonton to get some things I needed. When I got back, we were provided with accommodations in the Best Western in TaigaNova (at the north end of town).

About a week after Jen had left, she took our kids out to Newfoundland to stay with relatives.

It was three weeks before I saw Jen again, and even longer before I saw my kids.

It was tough doing the long distance thing. Some friends at Wandering River were kind enough to take our dogs for a couple of months.

Jen was called back to work, so she and I ended up staying with friends out at Saprae Creek, Gerald and Ruth, until we got things sorted out.

Elizabeth (artist)

I made it to Suncor's Millenium Camp. I had to stand for hours in line. During that time, I had a chance to visit with people around me. I talked to a couple in front of me about things, and it turned out we are all Christians. Also, someone brought me a plate of food. It tasted amazing. I was so tired from standing for hours and it being so late, yet I was very thankful when I was finally given a room.

In the morning, I woke up and showered. I felt so blessed to have had a bed to sleep in and to be able to shower. I decided to see what I should do after I ate breakfast.

On the way to the cafeteria, I was thinking about driving through Fort McMurray. I saw a fire truck and a firefighter. I asked if the highway was open. He said it was open for the time being.

I thought, 'I don't have enough gas… I don't know if I should attempt to leave'. I felt uneasy about doing the drive on my own. I imagined heavy traffic, so I decided to eat breakfast first and then try to head out.

A friend texted me that I should stay put. I also spoke with a man I knew from church. He said I should stay and wait. We exchanged ideas as to what we should do and what would happen.

After I finished eating, I headed to the security desk to find out if Highway 63 was open still. They said the RCMP said it was closed right then. I walked around and talked to Suncor staff to find out if they knew anything. I was told that the fire was heading north now and that we were going to be air lifted out later.

Visiting with another friend and her family, we chatted about our situation while watching TV news about the fire. Then the family decided that they were going to another work camp, further north, to be safe from the fire. Everyone was anxious.

I wasn't happy waiting while the fire drew closer. So once again, I went to check to see if the highway was open. At the security desk, they said the RCMP had opened the highway.

I thought, 'This is my chance to get out of here,' so I texted my brother-in-law and told him I was going to drive out and I would pick him up.

When I drove to his worksite a little further north, he was waiting at the side of the road. He was very thankful that I had come to get him. He didn't have anything with him, except his canvass lunch bag.

The highway was very quiet and I only saw a few vehicles here and there. It was smoky and warm. We went through a large cloud of smoke near Supertest Hill. Then it was clear again.

When we drove through Fort McMurray, we saw small fires smouldering, the city empty, and abandoned vehicles. Trees were burned and the place deserted. It looked like a war zone.

I looked at my gas gauge more and more the farther I drove, because I didn't have enough gas. I knew how much gas I needed to get to Wandering River. I knew I didn't have enough to get there, so I prayed that we would make it. My brother-in-law was emotional, and so was I. He wanted to turn the radio to CBC for news about what was happening, so we found the station.

My car was driving on empty for some time. I was surprised how far I could drive on an empty tank. I prayed again we would make it to get gas.

Finally, we saw a pickup truck at the side of the road. My brother-in-law knew the man who was there with his wife; he had worked with him. Sure enough they had free gas and snacks. We were very thankful for the snacks, and water and especially the gas, because I didn't know if there was any left at the station at Wandering River. We were relieved to make it to my sons' place in Bon Accord.

Katherine (quilter)

My in-laws, who under normal circumstances do not allow pets in their home, were very gracious. They have a large house with views of wooded areas (and therefore birds and other things of cat interest) out both their front and back windows. They had set aside their large utility room as a place for Moped to spend nights.

They were concerned that that she might get into the open ceiling as she does have that feat on her record. After checking for ways she might get up there, we determined it should not be a problem.

The next morning when we got up, we could not find the cat. Had we been wrong about her being able to get into the ceiling? After calling her a few times she came out of a hole in the wall she had found behind the dryer. It was not until later that we realized that their boiler makes a horrid noise when it kicks in, the kind that is the source of boogey man stories that keep kids from wanting to sleep in basements. We found another room for her and although she would cry and bang on the door whenever she heard anyone moving about, it worked reasonably well.

Moped settled in quite nicely. She had a huge house to roam (once we got the plants and a few special figurines out of her reach), lots of birds to watch, and double the normal staff to take care of her. She even started spending her afternoons watching farming videos with my father-in-law.

It turned out that Moped's evacuation adventures were not over. Halfway through our time away, we had to relocate to Edmonton. She took several more truck trips, sometimes packed below boxes, always with plenty of ventilation. She also got to live in a high rise with cardboard boxes for furniture, take her first elevator trip, find out that pigeons are not at all scared of her, go down 13 flights of steps and hang out in a parking lot due to a (thankfully false) fire alarm and discover that she is afraid of heights.

Michael (layperson)

At the camp where I stayed, I was able to share the gospel with people. I told them that suffering can open our hearts to God who meets us in our need, with mercy, grace, and salvation.

I was also able to gather people together to hear a short talk from the Bible about God's desire to be known by all people, and that in this time of difficulty, we could be used by him to bring everlasting hope to people around us. He WOULD do that if we were willing.

The people that joined us were moved and encouraged.

I posted this to Facebook, May 4th:

"The Lord my God never ceases to amaze me with His timing and sovereignty over all things.

I finally checked in at one of the nicest mining camps a person could ever imagine, stocked with food and even recreation for people to enjoy such as a movie theatre and billiards room.

And it dawned on me; "We are in the worst recession in some time... and as bad as that has been for our economy, had this fire been permitted to happen by God at any other time, these camps would probably be full, and the people of Fort McMurray would have nowhere to evacuate to."

Posted later, May 5th at the news that a friend's home in Abasand was spared.

"Oh, Heavenly Father, Lord of Hosts! We thank you for answering our prayer to protect the house of your children, Ivan and Beth! Praise be to God! So many miracles!

Fifty percent of the homes destroyed in my neighbourhood of Abasand and 574 are still standing. We may still have a chance at going home after all of this to help rebuild that city. Amazing! The house is surrounded by scorched earth. Amazing considering we are right on the green(ash) belt."

Around this time, my mother who had made it to Edmonton, had requested I come soon. I wasn't worried, plus I'd felt that the Lord wanted me to stay there to tend to people. I'd been able to share the gospel very clearly with one gentleman who seemed deeply moved. I'd invited him to go to his room (this is the afternoon of the 5th I believe) to pray in confession and accept forgiveness and surrender to the Lord and receive Christ.

He walked away fairly somber looking. An hour later he passed by all smiles. I don't know if it's because he prayed or not.

I should add, this happened because while the Suncor staff had set up tables with labels saying "Flights," "Toiletries," etc,

I sat at a small table, laid out tracts, and put up a label saying, "Prayer." And I did actually get to pray with a few people. I also had some female security guards come up. They perused the pamphlets, and one picked up one by LivingWaters.com "Why Does God Allow Suffering" and she'd commented, "This is something I'd like to understand," or something along the lines of that.

My response was to ask if she had any children. She didn't. I asked if she had any nieces or nephews. She did. I asked if she loved them. She did. I painted a scenario I commonly use where one of them at four or so years old was in the front yard, in the summer, dancing away eyes closed with headphones on, listening to their favourite jams. They're dancing towards the road. There's a large delivery truck cruising along and this little child is going to get hit and die. I asked what she would do. She said she'd be willing to run out and die in their place.

"Ahhh... now that's a response that will help us later. But what if that's not the option. What would you do?"

"I'd push them out of the way."

"You'd push them hard – forcibly – even though it could result in them being hurt on the pavement, maybe even resulting in life-altering brain injury?"

"Yes, I would if that's the choice."

Then I was able to respond, "God loves us so much that He will even allow difficulty in our life knowing it's such circumstances where we finally humble ourselves and turn to him." Then I shared the gospel, relating how as she would be willing to die for the children she loved, Christ died for us. She understood and was thankful for the chat and seemed visibly moved. Not sure what she did with the Gospel, but she did take a tract.

There was another fellow from the east coast that I invited to lunch along with others. He was on his own. By God's providence he was from my pastor's community back home and they knew each others' families. Anyway, I got to share the gospel with this fellow, too, and he talked a lot about straightening up and getting right. I tried to reiterate that it wasn't about doing or being good, but about surrendering to the Lord and growing a relationship. I think he understood. He sure looked convicted when he'd start thinking about that stuff, but I'd reassure him with the message of God's love.

Anyway, I told my mother I'd come when the Lord made it clear I had to leave, and not a minute earlier even if it meant being engulfed in flames with everyone else. She didn't like that but she understood.

That night at 10:45 pm, I shared something on Facebook from my good friend Pastor Neil from Anzac. He had shared a post by Kel:

Ok guys, difficult post. Fire is all around us. Crews are lining up along the Clearwater River attempting to protect the houses in lower townsite and the fire hall. The few fire fighters that are here at the hall are on the roof readying themselves to douse any embers. Me, I'm inside - all four dogs that remain with me are leashed and ready to flee to the truck at the last minute to head down the highway. Please pray wind and weather help out our brave men and women to beat this thing.

After that, I ran to the lobby and hollered for people to join me in prayer if not for their homes and the city, for the lives of the fire fighters. It was very dramatic. Kel's post sounded so dire, as if they were surround by fire a block away. I roused a number of people, probably thirty.

I felt bad. Some were Sikhs, others atheists no doubt, but nearly everyone respectfully stopped and prayed as I cried out to God. Was this the right thing to do? Maybe; maybe not.

Anyway, the next morning I woke up to a Suncor staffer banging on the door and unlocking it. "Time to go! We're all getting evacuated!!" It was very forceful and urgent sounding. I got ready quickly, went to the lobby, asked about flights, but the urgency was nowhere to be found out here. "I just had someone tell me we're being evacuated."

"No... If you can leave, we can assist you, but you can stay if you need."

I would hear later that once someone takes in an evacuee it's against the law to kick them out, which is why the first guy used deceit. Nevertheless, this seemed like the loud call of God to get out'a there. Who knows? Was my work done? Was there going to be a fuss about my late night prayer? I don't know, but I knew my mother wanted me to come to Edmonton.

I found out that convoys were going through town so I got in my car and by noon was on the road south. I was so thankful for the free fuel! It amazed me. Only ended up waiting in the convoy for a half hour before going on through town.

In Edmonton, I considered giving time to the Red Cross or somewhere else I could show Christ's love to people through service while sharing the Gospel as opportunities arose. But very quickly I felt that the Lord was saying, "This is time I'm giving you to work on your project. Focus on that." I praise him for that. He knew I needed time.

I was able to complete the organization of all my source material. It was a lot of work, but I began the final phase September 8th.

Anyway, Edmonton was nice. Got to spend time with family, and help plan some of the things our church could do on return. I was asked to help with the Distribution Centre that Rachel Ondang is in charge of and met with her to discuss plans. Due to the book, I had to say I could only commit limited time to helping it get together.

Meanwhile, the contractor I had worked for, who essentially 'rents out' heavy equipment operators to some of the larger oil companies, was being excellent in maintaining contact with us, giving us information so people wouldn't worry, etc. However, after a few days it was decided that they would lay us all off so we could receive unemployment. They promised that as soon as possible they would rehire us as contracts moved forward on the sites. This didn't help me much because I was not eligible for unemployment.

Elizabeth (artist)

My sons had a BBQ meal waiting for me and my brother-in-law when we arrived in Bon Accord. We really appreciated the hospitality. We were both shaken up from the evacuation. I didn't realize how shaken up I'd been until a week later, when I began to feel more like myself.

I was really concerned about my job and apartment, but my sons helped so much by being accommodating. I was not able to work as my families had spread all over the country.

My supervisor tried finding me more families to work with, but there were no families available. I decided to get involved with the local church. I joined the morning prayer meeting with the pastors. We prayed for all who had been evacuated, and I looked for work; but I didn't find anything suitable. I had to trust God about the future.

In the meantime, I decided to try and be a blessing to my children and grandchildren.

I went to church in Bon Accord mostly, with a wonderful pastor and congregation. One Sunday I decided to go to the Morinville Church where I met a wonderful couple. We talked for some time and they invited me to their home for lunch. I had prayed someone would invite me for lunch. God is good!

The husband encouraged me to use my gifts and gave me a book to read. I was amazed at how God provided just what I needed at that time.

Then I was invited to visit the Okotoks area. My middle son was in the process of moving there, and I was able to see his new home, my daughter-in-law and granddaughter, all whom I miss.

I was able to help them clean their kitchen. I didn't plan it but God made a way for me to be there to join in and be a part of their lives. My granddaughter and I had a wonderful time together playing and, then we all went out for dinner.

Back in Bon Accord at a prayer meeting, I met up with my friends at the Morinville church. Once again I was invited for lunch and we had wonderful fellowship. God is so good.

Thomas (father to seven children)

Being the oldest child, Allie took over caring for her siblings. Kindly, and gently hugging all of them before taking her seat, she then made sure all had water, and we headed off. I wasn't sure where we should be going, though. From the far reaches of my memory I recalled the little town of Waskatenau having a campground. And in Waskatenau I also had a friend. Maybe we could rest there. But it was south, and it was away from the fire. I urged the van onward.

The text from my friend Ken simply stated, "You can stay at the campground as long as you want. I've let the mayor know you're on your way."

I was starting to feel the stress, so the forty kilometre trip to Waskatenau seemed to take forever, but we finally made it. Turning the van into the campground entrance, there was a well taken care of baseball diamond to the left, and as the van slowly crept towards the one of six or seven campsites I saw Ken, waiting to guide us in. A familiar face, an understanding friend, and a kind heart are qualities that so many take for granted, myself included, and on that day, Ken was a godsend. I knew my family would be safe here. I knew that if I asked for anything, Ken would help. And I knew he would do it willingly and think nothing of it.

The business of backing the trailer in, getting levelled and hooked up took my mind all too briefly off of why we were here. The kids asked to go play in the field, and I was thankful that they didn't seem too traumatized. Their father however, was getting pretty messy inside.

As word spread of our arrival, the people from the town of Waskatenau and surrounding community reacted with kindness, grace, and as much help as was needed. Before long, people were streaming into our campsite with food, clothing, toys for the kids... it was overwhelming and I tried to thank each one personally and sincerely. Ken's daughter, Karen, took some command of the situation, organizing people and their offers of help. As I sat across from Ken at the picnic table, watching people I didn't even know coming to help us strangers and thankful for his kind heart, I once again had to choke down the tears, the raw emotion that wanted to consume every ounce of who I was. I wanted to scream, cry, laugh hysterically... or just melt. Instead, I gathered strength from knowing that I had the children to take care of. So, not yet, my pained heart. Not yet.

We settled in to Waskatenau. The school principal offered to let the kids attend classes. There was an outdoor movie night, and the kids were given popcorn and juice, toys were played with, and people came by, asking if there was anything else they could do help. They had all given so much, and it was uncomfortable declining that help, but we had more than enough in a very short time.

About two days into our stay, my youngest daughter, the bright blue-eyed, blonde haired bundle of energy known as Olivia was playing with a baby stroller next to a second stroller, close to the trailer when she suddenly started screaming. As I looked out the window, I saw her slowly getting to her feet, holding her stomach. I raced outside to find out what was the matter, only to find that she had fallen on the handle of the stroller and now had a deep gash in her belly. I picked her up as gently as I could, not wanting to cause more harm, and carried her to the trailer, laying her down carefully on the floor.

"Daddy, it really hurts!" she cried, and I was trying to be brave, and I was trying to stay calm, and I was trying to be the best Daddy ever. Try as I might a few tears fell as I yelled for someone to come help. There wasn't a lot of blood, but it was a deep, scary looking cut.

Almost as soon as I finished yelling, a nurse showed up at the door of the camper. I have no idea how, and then there was a first aid kit with another medic. Nurse told me that we would have to go to the hospital for stitches. Paramedic helped cover over the wound. I got into the van and tried to start it. The battery was dead. Another vehicle was brought immediately, and my blonde bundle and I got inside, about to leave.

"But what about the other kids?" I protested. Karen was there. "Go, we'll take care of them."

I muttered to Allie about being in charge, and as I was starting to pull away, Victoria, my second eldest, begged to come along and help. Jumping into the vehicle, she immediately started talking to my now strangely calm Olivia, distracting her from her pain.

I'm not sure how I got there, but we arrived at the Redwater medical centre. I carefully scooped up my beautiful little Olivia into my arms, the Daddy arms that couldn't stop her from getting hurt, and carried her in. We arrived at the desk, and the nurse asked for our Alberta Health Care.

"I'm sorry, but I just don't have it at the moment. We just got out of Fort McMurray."

That was all she needed to hear. We were whisked into an ER bed, and told that the doctor would be in shortly.

"Daddy, can you tell me a pretend story?" my little Olivia asked softly as she lay on that big bed, looking like the tiniest, bravest little girl I'd ever had the pleasure of knowing. Daddy had been given a job, and was happy for the distraction.

"Well, let's see... Once upon a time, there were four purple unicorns, and three pink unicorns. And they lived way up in a northern kingdom where people worked and played, and ate cotton candy all day long, and didn't have to eat green beans or peas or any of that yucky stuff. But there was a dragon that wanted to chase all the unicorns away! He breathed fire on anything he could, trying to get them to leave. And he almost won! But there was a princess that rescued three of the unicorns, and a daddy prince made sure they all got back together with all the other unicorns. And now, they get to go on a new adventure!"

As I was running out of unicorn ideas, the doctor came in to assess Olivia. Gently peeling back to bandage, it was decided that a combination of staples and stitches would be necessary. An IV was started, with Olivia bravely letting the staff do what was needed. A medication was given to help calm my baby girl, however it had the opposite effect. She started chatting at a million words a second, asking what does this do, and that, and can we go for ice cream? It was a welcome comedic break from the last few days.

Unfortunately, that comedy was all too brief, as the doctor came in scrubbed and ready to work. I knelt with my head close to my baby girl's whispering that it would be okay, and would be over soon, and the doctor has to do this to fix your belly. The crying, and the pleas from my sweet child to stop it from hurting turned into demands which were almost too much for this Daddy to handle. And then, sweet silence.

The Doctor was done, praised my little girl for being so brave, looked at me and said, "Dad, she'll be okay... and so will you." Then he left. We were free to go. My baby girl was bouncing to get out of there. And smiling.

We were just getting into the borrowed car when I received a call from the hospital. They informed me that there was someone that had heard the proceedings from the next bed, and was hoping to give us a gift. I agreed, and waited.

A professional looking woman walked out of the main entrance of the hospital a few moments later, making her way towards us. She had a calm, confident demeanour, with a kind face. I don't remember the whole conversation; I was too much of an emotional and mental mess. She is a kindergarten teacher in Redwater, and after hearing our story wanted to give us something to encourage us. She handed me a small blue paper gift bag, with bits of tissue paper poking playfully out the top. I moved the tissue paper aside to take hold of what us underneath. It was a small box.

Carefully opening it, those damn tears did in fact overwhelm me in front of this complete, beautiful stranger. She put her hand on my shoulder as I wept, offering kind words of empathy as big glistening tears streamed down my face.

Through clouded, teary vision I stared at the gift she had so thoughtfully given. Because you see, along with a wonderful inscription of hope, she had given us a hand crafted, gorgeous, one-of-a-kind, unicorn. And on a warm May day, in the middle of a hospital parking lot in Redwater, Alberta, Daddy cried. Over the next few days it wouldn't be the last time Daddy was overwhelmed with tears.

A day or so after the hospital, I was resting in the camper as the kids played outside, wondering when I would hear from my wife. She was due back in Canada anytime, and I could only imagine what kind of frantic a Mom would feel being thousands of kilometres away from her family while they were escaping a wildfire and not being able to do a single thing about it.

As I was just nodding off into a much needed nap, the phone rang. It was her! My lovely, beautiful wife!

"We're driving up that way right now. How are you? How are the kids? Do you have food? Water? Clothes? Is there anything we need?" She was immediately in Mom mode.

"We're okay, Honey. Really, we are." And that was all I could get out coherently after hearing my lovely's voice. I tried in vain to choke back sobbing tears, but couldn't. In all our years together, she had never heard that before. Daddy crying. Her tone softened to a lover's whisper. The kind that only two people deeply in love with each other can share.

Gently, softly... "It's okay, sweetheart. I'll be there soon. I love you."

I mustered a semi-coherent, "Okay..." and then hung up the phone. Would she think I was weak? Too soft? Too mushy?

The hour or three before she got to Waskatenau were the three longest hours I've spent waiting for someone. I was anxious to see her, and nervous at the same time. Did I do it right? Did I do what Dads are supposed to? Would she still think I was "her man"?

As those thoughts swirled around in my mind, I saw her father's truck pulling into the campground from the picnic table I was sitting at. Standing up, I tried to straighten and groom the borrowed clothes I'd been given, trying to make myself as presentable as possible.

It's hard to describe how a soul mate makes you feel. The fresh breath that comes with seeing the one you have loved more than anyone on this earth after what seems like an eternity apart.

As my wife got out of the truck, anxiety was replaced by calm, nervousness replaced by peace, fear replaced with hope. Not a word was spoken as we drew close to each other. None were necessary. We were together. And as my lovely put her arms around my neck and gently pulled me close, I knew we would be alright. Somehow, some way, in spite of that damned fire, we would be okay.

And Daddy wept.

Trish (storyteller)

Wednesday, May 4th

7:00 am

Warren texts to say that there is lots of bacon. I shower and join the others for breakfast. We go for a walk. My friends are anxious to get to YEG. CNRL staff set up a table and take names for a flight. I am reluctant until they say I can take Cokie in his cage, on my lap. We pack, we wait; we recharge phones, watch CBC.

11:00 am

We are bused to the CNRL landing strip; wait some more; board the plane. There are five Canadian North 737's waiting; the scale of this place (new word: "aerodrome") is huge. We wait some more and board the plane. Cokie has never flown before; he is calm, preens his feathers the whole time. Good boy. I've never seen a quieter airplane.

2:30 pm

We get to YEG; the volunteers have food and beverages waiting. Warren leaves; no luggage for Auni and Ermias. We wait. Shelley (Calgary) texts and calls, and gets us in touch with her family's friends, Doni and Jay (Edmonton), who are able to take me and Auni in as long as we need.

7:30 pm

Doni and Jay pick us up as Auni is getting her luggage; Ermias stays to wait for his luggage and his friends. They take us home, we drink a lot, and we go to bed.

Thursday, May 5th

2:30 am

I am ill and hung over. After two days of constipation, I plug the toilet--ARE YOU KIDDING ME??

6:30 am

Up early; nauseated and throbbing head and terribly embarrassed. Doni is wonderful; makes me toast so I can get down an Advil; attacks the plugged toilet successfully. I shower. Cokie is okay. Good boy. We watch the news and I book a flight to Comox. I need my parents.

3:00 pm

Need to get a pet carrier for Cokie's WestJet flight. Doni lends us her RAV-4; it's a stick shift. I can't drive stick, but Auni can. We set out together on errands: we hit AMA, two banks, and PetSmart, and get back to Doni and Jay's in time for BBQ burgers.

Friday, May 6th

YEG has smoke from the north. Auni arranges to meet her sister. We say our goodbyes. I shove Cokie into the pet carrier and he freaks out. SHUT UP COKIE. I shove in his mirror and he calms immediately. Doni drives me to the airport.

Everyone wants to meet Cokie. I meet a lot of Fort McMurray people in the security lineup. I board the plane and have a nap. Cokie stays silent the whole trip.

Mom and Dad are waiting in Comox; I break down when I hug Mom. We drive to Qualicum Beach. Everything here is green and in flower. I am in shock.

I talk to Pam: her house is burned to the ground. Christel's house is gone too. No one else knows for sure just yet. They all made it out, though. Sarah and Kevin also made it to YEG; Lisa made it to her trailer in Wandering River; David is near Lac La Biche. Linda is still at Shell Albion with her mom.

Saturday May 7th – Wednesday June 8th

Cokie and I stay with my parents in Qualicum Beach. I eat, sleep, watch the news. I watch every press conference and listen to every telephone town hall.

I see Linda when she finally gets back to the island. I even get to see Amalis; we laugh about boy problems vs. forest fire problems. Mostly, I just watch, listen, and wait.

JD (radio announcer & reporter)

I was stressed about the future. I didn't know anything at that point. I worked through the first two and a half weeks-- watching social media and doing interviews with Global News, CTV News, Globe & Mail, MacLean's magazine, and other news outlets, and radio stations across Canada. I felt like God gave me the ability to do my job even though I didn't know if we had a radio station.

At about 4:30 pm on May 3rd, the radio station had gone dead. We thought it was because the station burned down, but we found out later that the electrical power to Downtown had been turned off.

This year we had put up a brand new 40,000 watt tower near the old airport. It withstood about $40,000 worth of damage which was not insured.

Saturday June 4th, I was able to put the station back on the air remotely. It was a beautiful moment. There were challenges and yet God was meeting the need. We were able to program the station and be on the air.

During those weeks of displacement, I was at peace through the first part of it. There was a sense of camaraderie with the slogan, 'Fort McMurray Strong'.

Dee (poet)

After a shower and change of clothes, I watched the news with my brother-in-law John and his wife Jo. I felt sick to my stomach from the images: buildings burning, evacuees pouring into evacuation centres in Lac La Biche and Edmonton. Chief Darby kept us updated.

A news station had seen my tweet and requested an interview. A little while later, I was on TV remotely, trying to explain what our escape felt like, how my husband was stuck at work, and why people were running out of gas and abandoning their vehicles.

My husband phoned from work. We spoke briefly and he told me he hadn't slept much, wondering how we were making out, happy now that we were safe. I worried about him. The fire was headed north. Were the oil sands operations safe? When could he come and join us? He didn't know. My sister had safely sheltered for the night at the Suncor camp. Others hadn't found room and were camped at the side of the highway in tents if they had them, or they slept in their vehicles.

As people awoke, the traffic picked-up while some continued further north to work camps and others took their chances by heading south, hoping the highway was open.

We were glued to the news and social media. We prayed for the firefighters, RCMP officers, and others working in the area, such as the Water Treatment Facility staff who remained on duty despite mandatory evacuations to provide firefighters with water.

We, along with many others, told them they could enter our houses for food and anything else they might need. We left them messages on social media, asking them to stay safe as their lives were more important than our homes.

Our family said to stay as long as we needed. Other relatives offered places. Our grown children stayed with their cousin Mike and his wife Melissa nearby. We weren't accustomed to being needy.

Our son Aaron took his dog to the vet. After a thorough exam and X-ray, the vet declared he didn't owe a thing. Restaurants gave free meals, clothing stores slashed prices and gave evacuees discounts. People offered free shared accommodations, and even the use of unoccupied campers, houses, apartments, and more.

Everywhere we went in Edmonton, we saw other Fort McMurrayites, dazed; thankful to be alive; full of stories about their escape. No-one knew what would happen. The news confirmed heavy loss in several areas; but great hope that most of the city would be okay.

Evacuees trickled into Edmonton for days, by car, bus, and plane, eventually emptying the camps which had miraculously been almost vacant with the downturn in the economy.

Some residents had nowhere to go except the Evacuation Centres. Many were new immigrants to Canada. There was a despondency in the centres as a gastrointestinal bug spread among 105 people.

Donations of all types poured into central collection spots and displaced families lined up for hours to select clothing, soap, deodorant, baby food, a towel from the piles. There were too many items to mention, but pet food was there, drinking water, and piles of toiletries of every sort.

Edmonton was buzzing as it filled to capacity. It was too loud, too busy. Friends said to open an insurance claim. How long would we be out of our home? Had we lost our home? How badly was it damaged? We didn't know. We were given a small advance on insurance to help with immediate needs.

Residents in Slave Lake began offering advice on Facebook-- expect to be out at least a month. Don't open your fridge when you go home. Keep all your receipts. No, it can't be true, I thought. We'll be home in a few days. We continued to binge-watch news and social media. Our anxiety continued to increase.

On Mother's Day Sunday, my adult kids took me to a nearby church. The pastor said he had planned a sermon, but today he felt he needed to stray from it, and teach about dealing with anxiety.

His first PowerPoint slide had a paraphrase: "Don't worry about anything; instead, pray about everything. Tell God what you need, and thank him for all he has done."

At the end of the sermon, a prayer was displayed, and everyone was instructed to pray along, out loud.

"God, take control of my mind and help me to think on things that are true, honourable, right, pure, lovely, and admirable."

He felt he should pray specifically for three people. (My two kids and me?) I felt my anxiety lesson. I felt God's peace wash over me.

After a week in the city, we felt we had to get away and find a quiet place to unwind. By then, all the places in and around Edmonton were taken. Chloe found us a pet-friendly rental in the country near Calgary, so we headed off, pets and all. We made a point of turning off the TV most of the time; of looking at the scenery and enjoying the mountain view. We were also closer to our youngest at his temporary school. We were able to visit with him more often. He was unhappy.

We visited a church in a town where we were invited for lunch; a lady tried to push money into my hands; we were welcomed and prayed for from the pulpit; and a business owner offered us a free apartment in Calgary for two months. But we were comfortable in our little rental in the country.

Friends from Calgary came to visit us and brought us a meal. The friendly people of small towns outside Calgary were always compassionate and welcoming, sometimes refusing payment or giving us discounts. We were often moved to tears; they called us victims of a disaster, and they knew what it was like. Many of them had come through the flood in High River three years earlier.

As the fire continued ravaging the northern boreal forest in and around Fort McMurray, wind gusts would send it in several directions at once. It continued to make progress north, and all of a sudden, oil sands operations were evacuating workers and shutting down the plants.

It was the first time that entire plants would be shut down, since they'd begun operations. Would they start up again smoothly? How long would it take?

Would the entire plant burn to the ground leaving us without our main source of income? I suddenly felt as though everything we had worked for could disappear.

There were rumours circulating that insurance companies would go bankrupt with the magnitude of claims from residents. It was difficult to know what was true.

We visited several churches during our displacement. Each time, the music would flow in and around us. I felt God comforting, healing. My anxiety lessened and I believed that whatever happened, even if our house was completely gone, even if the oil sands mines and plants closed, we were going to be okay.

My son Aaron and his friend Ian made their way south to Lethbridge where his girlfriend attended university for summer session. A realtor found them a rental. When she heard they were from Fort McMurray, people brought over furniture and kitchen supplies for the young men to use. My mother's heart was comforted.

Reports about which houses still stood, and which had burned down completely slowly trickled out. Some friends from Beacon Hill still had homes standing while others had total loss. Everyone we knew in Waterways had total loss, as did a few families in Saprae Creek. Not as many lost homes in Thickwood and Timberlea, but most had varying degrees of smoke damage.

My heart ached for those traumatized by the escape, and I felt overwhelmed by the stories of complete loss. But the worst news came when we heard about a young man, Aaron Hodgson and his cousin, Emily Ryan who had been killed on impact from a head-on collision on Highway 881. In horror, Emily's grandparents, mother Melonie, and other family members who were all traveling in a caravan, watched the vehicle engulfed by explosions and flames, unable to save them. Hadn't we all prayed for the safety of everyone fleeing?

Would this family have the faith of Job to withstand this trial? I hoped so.

The Government of Alberta and the Red Cross took donations and distributed funds to every person displaced. Samaritan's Purse from Calgary took a tractor-trailer of supplies and volunteers north to the city, to be ready on site for re-entry.

Other charities and agencies went into help mode, doing whatever was necessary. Facebook groups became places of support, prayer, and encouragement, as well as a place to vent. A new phrase was coined: "evac fat", as many of us gained weight eating as a means of comfortable routine, anxious and uncertain about the future.

However, people began sharing inspiring stories with me.

Several fire fighters had fought the Beast to save homes and businesses while their own homes burned to the ground. Pharmacist David Hill had remained in Fort McMurray, providing prescription medications to people working in the city, as well as those evacuated to camps. He was one of the many people compelled to stay, despite personal danger.

A dog musher took her team of sled dogs to MacDonald Island where others provided dog food and more, only to be later sent out of town.

Family friends were quickly packing items in their home in Waterways, when a friend driving by noticed their back fence catch fire from the blaze directly behind their house, causing him to stop and pound on their door, insisting they leave. They immediately did, escaping through flames.

Our MLA Brian Jean lost his home in Waterways. It was his second personal tragedy since one of his sons had passed away early in the year. Yet Brian stood next to others who were struggling, lending support.

Then there were the men who stayed behind in Saprae Creek where the fire went through erratically, trying to save their neighbours' homes.

In addition, many pets had been left behind when owners were told to flee directly from work. Volunteers, including Howard a locksmith, entered homes to feed and care for pets, then sent them out of town to be re-united with their owners.

Stories continued to spread; good news to warm our hearts.

A couple of weeks later, a friend mentioned how he'd asked the cable company to ping his modem to see if it was still active. I decided to phone Shaw, our internet provider. They were able to ping our modem, and assurance came back: yes, it pinged. Our modem was working. The power was on; our house was okay.

The Government of Alberta released aerial images of the Wood Buffalo Region, sent to residents who had registered with the Red Cross. We were able to zoom in and see our home, before the fire, and after. We could see a massive firebreak where trees on the Birchwood Trails had been bulldozed. We were very thankful; our hearts again breaking for those who had lost their homes.

Our new normal in southern Alberta was to wonder each day when and if the oil sands plants would restart. We, along with everyone else who had registered with the Red Cross, began receiving Town Hall phone calls from Mayor Blake and heads of the assembled fire and recovery team.

Each day, if we chose, we could listen to a Town Hall update and possible re-entry details. Many days we didn't listen because it would bring on stress. We tried to tune out of social media and television, keeping our exposure to a minimum, to help us heal.

There was much happening in regards to the fire, but at the forefront of our minds was always our youngest son. The idea of providing a better situation for him stuck and we began to look for a place in Southern Alberta. One without trees. We spent quite a bit of time looking, but couldn't find anything.

On my birthday in mid-May, I woke to a gloomy, wet day. My husband and I went to an insurance office to ensure our coverage hadn't lapsed. Next door was a cupcake cafe, so we went in for a birthday treat. I commented on how cute the café was, and the owner asked where we were from. When we told her, her face fell and she gushed sympathy, saying,

"It's on me". I couldn't stop crying while I sipped my coffee and ate the cupcake.

Certain words and reactions triggered us and made us feel like victims. "Let's not tell anyone anymore that we're from Fort McMurray," I said.

Our young son stayed with us weekends there, and our dogs, Cay and O'Malley provided comic relief as they learned to dig for gophers and run with the resident horses.

A local Border Collie enjoyed teasing O'Malley, and they'd chase and play for hours, enjoying the Alberta foothills. The lizard, Stubbs, didn't mind his smaller terrarium. We let him run around the floor sometimes, even though we lost him occasionally and needed to search on our hands and knees, being careful where we stepped.

Our upstairs neighbour mentioned a few times that he'd like to start a fire in the backyard firepit to roast sausages and marshmallows with us, before we left. My husband's eyes blazed, but he said nothing. He later told me he could not enjoy a fire now; it used to be one of his favourite things when we camped.

Near the start of June, my husband left to return to work in the north with a boil-water advisory in effect, while I stayed south with our daughter. He lovingly did the initial house clean-up with a kit and instructions provided by the Red Cross. A part of me did not want to go back at all. It was beginning to feel like home in the south. I had been content in Fort McMurray, but we wanted to do whatever it took to help our son succeed.

I looked at open houses and found a realtor to work with. At a church in Calgary one Sunday, a lady prayed with me; among other things, she prayed God would provide the right house for us.

At the end of June, once the boil-water advisory was lifted, I returned to Fort McMurray.

Alisa (engineer)

We unloaded the kids, dogs, and luggage into the small room at Mildred Lake Camp. We finally had time to call loved ones and to process what had just happened.

Luckily, we had enough gas to leave the next morning before the highway was closed. We spent a night in Athabasca with friends and then continued on to Calgary, where we stayed for the next five weeks.

When I think back to that day, May 3rd, I am thankful our city is full of smart, practical, calm people. We live 500 km from anywhere, but miraculously, got ourselves out. When we did, the rest of Alberta was there to welcome us with gas, water, and hugs. But the credit for our safe evacuation belongs with regular people, doing ordinary jobs, under extra-ordinary circumstances.

Cyndy (composer)

The rest stop was packed. We set up our sleeping quarters and Al hit the hay. He was exhausted. Faith went to bed, but I felt compelled to wait up for the boys. They arrived from Anzac at 2:40 am. with 30 litres of diesel fuel. It was all they could get. The line-ups for fuel had been just as crazy in Anzac as Fort Mac. In all we had travelled approximately 100 kilometres.

Everyone bedded down and slept until 7 am. Al went to survey the situation while I made breakfast. We had no place to be and no rush to get there. Someone Al met gave him some fuel and with that and what the boys brought, we were ready for the next leg of our journey. Al found a lady who needed gasoline and we gave her some from the generator in the RV. She stayed for breakfast. It was good to help one another as we shared a common experience of disaster.

But we were not expecting the outpouring of love and concern from people outside of Fort Mac. We commented to each other many times over, how kind and generous everyone was. People drove north from Edmonton, Gibbons, Calgary, and so many places I'd never heard of, bringing fuel, water, food and encouragement as we traveled south.

The traffic continued at a snail's pace. We left Mariana Lake at 9 am and arrived in Grassland at 3 pm- that's normally about an hour and 40 minutes drive. We hoped to fuel up in Grassland, but the stations were packed and maneuvering with our RV was out of the question. Someone on the side of the road sold us $15 of fuel and we journeyed on.

We reached Boyle around 4 pm, an hour to drive about 30 kilometres. We got a full tank of fuel for the first time in our flight. From there to Andrew and Rose's farm was another three hours or so of driving. We had to stop for a few supplies since the farm was quite remote. We finally arrived at our home away from home at 9 pm.

Our whole family was reunited on the farm as we waited out our evacuation. Several friends also enjoyed the Barley's hospitality as they waited to return home. It was a time of uncertainty, but speaking only for myself I must say that it was a time of great blessing for me. Our family was together in a way that we haven't been for some time. We were able to help Andrew and Rose with some of the work on their farm. We were able to visit with friends in southern Alberta and enjoy the blessings of God through so many people who stepped in to help us. Barbara White spearheaded a group from around Winfield, a small town near the farm, who brought us food, clothes, bedding, and most of all welcomed us into their community.

We had dinner at the Legion and an evening of visiting and desserts. The Sharp families who own several farms near "ours" were the epitome of good farm neighbours. We made real friends while we were evacuated.

We were involved in a car accident on Mother's Day, 5 days after evacuation. But even there we saw the good hand of our God upon us. Neither we nor the ladies in the other vehicle were seriously injured. They were generous and gracious to us, refusing to press charges. Our truck was eventually repaired and the insurance covered the rental vehicle.

Al was able to continue working out of Calgary and we got a preview of what it would be like for him to fly in and out of work if we left Fort McMurray.

Joe (RCMP & Harley rider)

A friend of mine, a business owner, in the community where I live had contacted me and said he and other business people and friends had put together some supplies to take back to Fort McMurray for the emergency personnel. I hauled a pick-up truck full of energy bars, soft drinks, snacks and toiletries back. An overwhelming gesture, and much needed since some provisions were scarce in the early days of the fire for emergency personnel.

It's funny how my little go bag became such a convenience and a real luxury to me in the first days of my deployment. Many others who had been forced from their homes had nothing. The Operations Officer I worked alongside when I first went to Fort McMurray had the uniform he was wearing and nothing else. It seems funny how a toothbrush and toothpaste can give so much comfort.

The transformation of the city was remarkable to me. When I lived there it was hustle and bustle, things in motion at all hours of the day; most people moving about with a purpose and of course some moving about without a purpose, but moving all the same.

After leaving the city where my wife grew up, the beauty of such a place really came out. The shock of the devastation certainly brings back the things you did and the good memories attached to them.

I was back and forth to Fort McMurray four times to serve the community during the month of May, and was there to see the city transform and return to life; at least as much as it could at that time.

On my second deployment to Fort McMurray, I worked nightshift for eight nights and had an opportunity to travel the community as part of my duties. I patrolled the burned out communities and found my friend's property in Waterways.

He is a fellow motorcycle enthusiast. His home was reduced to a layer of ashes in the basement which now held kitchen appliances standing upright, below where they once were positioned in the happy kitchen.

In what was once the garage sat the remains of an anniversary edition Harley Davidson motorcycle, like an apparition of the underworld. It too was reduced to a frame and a few recognizable parts sitting upright.

I can say without embarrassment, there were times I had tears in my eyes driving around wondering what life would be like for people who lost their homes; wondering how someone can recover from such a tragedy. It's not all about the loss of a home or some possession we acquire along the way.

It is about the memories within, irreplaceable things such as photographs of loved ones who have passed on and the memories the photographs hold. It's also about the emotional trauma of rebuilding life.

I'm not going to take away from anyone who didn't lose a home and the emotional trauma the wildfire caused for them. I, too, walked away from my experience being affected by it.

I was there when everyone was fleeing. I saw the community a literal ghost town. It is a strange and eerie feeling driving through the city at night; some areas without power, therefore no street lights, smoke thickly hanging in the air and the remains of homes and vehicles in my headlights, all ghostly reminders of the community where children were playing and people were going about their business.

On my third tour back in Fort McMurray, although fires continued in the city and the fires outside the city continued to threaten, I started noticing the beginnings of rebirth. The city population was reduced to emergency and essential personnel so it was virtually deserted. This is the time when Emergency Operations had already begun planning for infrastructure to return so that residents could return.

PART VI
RETURN TO
FORT MCMURRAY

Joe (RCMP & Harley rider)

Mother Nature was first. I noticed grass growing in areas that had been burned, as if by magic. One day the ground was black and burned out, the next day the most beautiful green that grass could be was emerging through the ash.

As necessary infrastructure was allowed to come back to the city to begin clean up and prepare for the return of people, the city slowly came to life. At one point early after the evacuation you could fire a cannon down Franklin Avenue without hitting anything; now much more traffic was there. Not the heavy, time delaying traffic most people were used to, but at least there was evidence life existed.

I was there when the first residents began arriving in the city. Although we were preparing for a flood of vehicles, it really wasn't like that. But all the same it was good to see people returning.

Members (of the RCMP) were manning posts along the way and getting waves, thumbs up, and honking of horns as a show of thanks and gratitude for our service to the community.

Christina (public relations)

It's been tough living without (my husband) these past few weeks and our future is so uncertain.

We lost everything in that fire and I am left to care for my boys and plan a birth by myself.

My oldest son is having nightmares but he's been slowly getting better. He just wants to go home like the rest of us.

Danelle (work-at-home mom)

Five weeks later, Drew had to return to Fort McMurray to work and stay in camp for a week. That was the hardest goodbye I've ever experienced.

That agonizing week apart solidified that we would do everything we could to not have to be apart.

When it was time for Drew to again go north, we returned to Fort McMurray as a family on June 21st.

I was amazed at how much it felt like returning home, even though we couldn't return to our house.

Trish (storyteller)

Thursday, June 9th

10:30 am

Leave Comox (and Cokie); fly to Calgary. Shelley (Calgary) takes a break from Customs to meet me and I break down.

2:00 pm

Must take taxi to another terminal to board Canadian North charter back to CNRL; construction delays, then dropped at wrong building. SURELY YOU MUST BE JOKING.

Run to correct building in searing hot sun. Make my flight; land at CNRL aerodrome in pouring rain.

5:30 pm

Must pee but don't know where. Follow crowd to waiting buses; none say "Joslyn"; ask around, and one driver offers to drop me there after he does his usual run.

We travel down every pot-holed, wash-boarded gravel road at CNRL before reaching Joslyn. MUST FIND BATHROOM NOW.

Grateful to find that car will start. I have enough gas to get to town.

I go home in pouring rain. It screens the devastation.

8:00 pm

Home is like a time capsule. No power loss, so very little spoiled food (the bacon, unfortunately). A study in contrasts, with what I'd been seeing in the media.

It is nothing short of miraculous.

Dee (poet)

I'd seen the images on the news and on Facebook. The sign at the side of the highway as you drive into Fort McMurray normally reads: "Welcome to Fort McMurray". City workers had replaced the "To" with "Home", so it read, "Welcome Home Fort McMurray".

Other signs lined the boulevard: Thank You for Staying Safe; Thank you for Being Resilient; We will Rebuild; and more. It was difficult to read the signs and drive with wet, blurry vision.

Returning to Fort McMurray felt surreal. I was afraid to put down my window. I switched my car intake to 'recirculate' to keep the smoky smell out. I was returning home, but this was now an in-between time.

Friends came and went, too busy to visit. Everyone had cleanup and insurance to deal with, trips to Edmonton to replace items, family holidays and house hunting. My husband cleaned thick ash off the outside of the house and from our yard, and I needed to replace our patio furniture cushions.

There were no fireworks in Fort McMurray for Canada Day that July.

Of my closest friends, four out of eight would move away. We were used to goodbyes; now it was our turn to say it.

On another trip south a week later, I finally found a place. It wasn't perfect; a fixer-upper. It would be our Southern Alberta home. Our youngest son would be with us there. It wasn't a perfect plan, but it was our miracle; one we didn't see coming.

David (firefighter with three sons)

We found a house for rent in Dickinsfield for a while. Jen was very pregnant when all this happened; she was six months pregnant when the fire occurred; then the kids came back in July and things began to settle. We started to go through the insurance process. We lived out of suitcases.

The blessings during that time were incredible. We had so many people helping us and supporting us; it was humbling.

So many people said, "Hey because you lost so much, we want to help you out." It was incredible.

I've never been on the receiving end of peoples' generosity like that. It was truly humbling to be blessed that way.

Everything just fell into place. We were staying in Dickinsfield at a nice place. The insurance process was quite strange; it was more beneficial to us financially to take a payout and purchase another property than rebuild, so we decided to take that route.

JD (radio announcer & reporter)

I was fine for the first weeks, and then it turned into a month. Re-entry week came.

I went back to Fort McMurray with my sister and found my home without even the smell of smoke.

That was the incredible providence of God for that portion of the city, and the incredible work of the first responders.

Katherine (quilter)

After six and a half weeks of new adventures, we all came home and several contractor visits later, things for Moped, were back to normal.

She can go out in the backyard, watch her birds, and sleep in all her favourite places. Oh, and we now have a boarder, or as she prefers to view him, another person to pet her.

Michael (layperson)

On June 6th I returned. I was blown away by how beautifully green everything was.

I entered the lobby of my apartment. A little smoky smelling. I took the elevator to my third floor. Less smoky. I entered my unit. I couldn't smell smoke at all. I'd had the presence of mind to ensure all my windows were closed and that my AC/heating unit was off so no outside air would circulate into my place. It smelled fine.

I opened the fridge. Living as a single bachelor, busy with ministry work rather than spending hours preparing fancy meals, it was relatively barren. Just a litre of spoiled milk I could throw out. A quick washing and it would be fine.

Then I was off to assist Rachel Ondang at church as that place became an awesome distribution centre for airplane hanger loads of donations. We could share God's love by providing for others. I spent every day there for nearly a week sorting things out, and then less and less as time went on.

While in Edmonton, probably late May, I'd received an email from my previous employer– an "e-sign" letter where you can open it and electronically sign your signature on the document. I assumed this was for me to go back to work. Now all I had to do was be patient.

End of June, the bank account was getting scarce again. I was so grateful for my one and only paycheque for four days work with the company I'd been hired with before the evacuation; the Red Cross money; and the government debit card.

As well, DirectEnergy had withheld billing for three months, and the banks deferred my mortgage and my line of credit and my credit card. That was amazing! But it was getting close to when I would have to pay again.

PART VII
RECOVERY

JD (radio announcer & reporter)

December, 2016

We lost two staff members who did not return. One is still in the hospital now (end of November 2016), and we pray God would continue to heal her.

God opened so many doors through this. I spoke in schools and youth groups in Central Alberta and told how God saved me and protected me. It was incredible to see students who were also displaced, to encourage them, and give them hugs, to say, we will be okay.

I returned to Fort McMurray on June 27th and began work on June 28th. It started a month and a half of intense deep depression, stress and anxiety. I had survivor's guilt.

On July 1st, I went into Abasand with a good friend of mine who lost his home, and something broke inside me. As I mentioned earlier, I lived in Abasand for nine months. When I saw what Abasand looked like, I physically felt something break inside me. That weekend, I did not leave my bed. I cried and I cried, and I contemplated suicide as the stress, anxiety, and depression hit me like a big tsunami wave.

At about 4 pm on Sunday, I got out of bed and I went back to work Monday morning. I tried to play it off like everything was okay. I wanted to be 'Fort McMurray Strong', but I didn't realize that by trying to be strong I was only hurting myself.

For the next month and a half, I had four bouts when thoughts of suicide almost caused me to end my life. The fourth bout was the worst, and as I was about to drive off and do it, my mom called me and said she'd felt the Holy Spirit tell her to phone me because she knew something was wrong. She asked me if I was okay, and when I said "No," she knew she'd needed to call me. We talked and then I went home to sleep.

Eventually, the middle of August came and I went home to Central Alberta to see my family, and to attend the No Greater Love music festival. God healed me that weekend in a really big way.

I thank God for bringing me through the stress, anxiety, depression, and suicidal thoughts. I still deal with stress and anxiety to this day, but because of what God has done, I have been able to see how to get through it. Through this, I have been able to talk with others about their depression, their stress, their anxiety, their bouts of suicidal thoughts, and I've been able to share how God protected me, how God guided me, how God led me; and that spoke to others.

On Sunday November 28th, I spoke along with others in a team of seven young adults in my church about the experience. I reminded the church that it's okay not to be 'Fort McMurray Strong'. Because we aren't Fort McMurray strong. In our weakness, God is strong, which it says in 1 Corinthians (in the Bible).

We don't need to be Fort McMurray Strong; we need to be God Strong, and rely on the strength that God provides in the hardest, the toughest, and the most impossible situations.

Through this whole thing, I have seen God take me from the brink of death five times within several months, and lead me through it. No matter how weak you feel today, know that in your weakness, His strength will come to you. When there is no way, He will make a way.

Christina (public relations)

January 2017

We are doing great.

We are in Fort McMurray, staying in a rental in Timberlea while our house is being rebuilt. Our foundation was poured in October and our rebuild is progressing nicely. We hope to be back in our home early summer.

The boys are good and the baby is growing quickly.

Wina (backcountry enthusiast)

When we returned to Fort McMurray, my husband Chris and I attended the only church that was open. They asked for volunteers to work with Samaritan's Purse, so my husband and I said we'd help.

My job was to talk to the homeowners and try to keep them calm while the men laboured getting fridges and freezers out of their house. The smell from most of them was hard to handle.

One lady we helped was telling us her husband had died a few months earlier. We hugged; actually we hugged just about everyone.

One lady told us her 12-year-old son was separated from her for two days before they could get to him. He was so mad at his parents.

One BIG man was quite quiet. He didn't talk too much while everyone emptied his fridge (which smelled so bad). Then he told me, his brother lived around the corner; he'd lost his house all together. (He started to cry.)

One house was used by renters. The amount of dead flies in it was horrendous. The boys had to take doors off to get both fridge and freezer out. Maggots were falling out of the fridge. That was a hard one, but the owner was so nice, and really appreciated the help.

One lady told us how she and her husband were running from the flames, the clothes on their backs burning.

Afterwards, we handed each home owner or renter a copy of the Holy Bible, "personally signed by each of us there to help".

Then we huddled around the person, and prayed for them. Most people were very receptive, wanted the prayers, wanted the Bible and really appreciated the help. Only one person turned down the Bible but still allowed us to pray.

My husband and I did this for four days. It was rewarding, and yet personally draining.

Mary (pseudonym)

"The Lord giveth and the Lord taketh away. Blessed be the name of the Lord." Job 1:21 KJV

These were the last words from my husband's mouth as we climbed into our truck expecting that we would never see our house, and possibly our community, again.

Those words are often used in times of tragedy or in the face of imminent loss. The focus is usually on what is being taken away. It is a way to remind ourselves that we and all we have belong to God, part of His greater plan. My husband and I tried to mentally prepare ourselves for great loss. But in its own way, God's giving has had its own challenges.

In most ways, our experience of the Fort McMurray wildfires was a best-case scenario. My husband was able to get home from work before we had to leave. We had time to pack before heading out. We never drove through fire. We had a roof over our heads every night. We never went without food or water. We had somewhere to go. When we had to relocate part way through the evacuation, all those needs were provided for as well. My husband's job was secure and we never missed a paycheque.

When we returned home, our house just needed a clean. We didn't have to fight with our insurance company. Through it all we had the support of friends, family and wonderful strangers.

A couple of months after returning to town, my Bible Study group got together to share our experiences. One had lost her house; the rest had returned to situations similar to my own. No one had lost their jobs. And although there were challenges and the initial days of escape were tough, we had all landed into the loving hands of family or friends.

Every woman present would say without a shadow of a doubt that God had His hand in their voyage, that it was only by God's grace that no one died in that fire, that He was present in all those difficult moments.

Yet I noticed other things. Although they did not say it outright, or perhaps even fully realize it, every wife was mad at her husband. The reasons were mostly beyond the men's control. Work kept some from their families in those first critical hours and days. Some families lived in situations not of their choosing while others were separated for weeks. Many of these women felt they bore the brunt of keeping the family and household safe, together and running.

I'm sure the men were dealing with their own challenges from being separated from their families and unable to just fix things.

In addition to these challenging situations, my friends and I were suffering from fear and anxiety that could be triggered by anything and often by nothing. We weren't sleeping well. We battled survivor's guilt on an ongoing basis.

These types of feelings and raw emotions went well beyond our small group throughout the people of Fort McMurray, both those who had returned and those who remained away. Many who had lost their homes or could not yet move back expressed anger towards those who had a house to live in. They felt forgotten and that the rest of the city was moving on without them.

Those who could live in their houses felt like they were not allowed to have or express their own emotions. Any troubles they had were trivial and not worthy of mention. One post stabbed my heart. "If you have not lost everything you do not have a right to an opinion." The pain behind that post is overwhelming; the pain it caused was widespread and long-lasting.

I felt stuck within an environment of physical and emotional chaos. I told myself that I shouldn't feel anger, fear, or anxiety because nothing bad had happened to me. Regardless, as a Christian, wasn't I supposed to give thanks in everything? Wasn't I failing, even sinning, if I felt fear? Frustration? Discouragement?

I have since thrown away the lie that nothing bad happened to me yet there are times I still feel stuck. I fully believe that

God is in control and that He has a plan for using all that has and continues to happen.

Yet even as I glimpse pieces of that plan coming into place, I still struggle with fear. I still have problems falling asleep. I am wary of where and how I talk about what God has given me because I don't understand why I came back to my home while many of my friends did not.

Recently my father-in-law was telling me about a conference he had gone to. The point that stuck with me was bringing glory to God. Whatever we want, whatever we do, whatever we pray for, should have the purpose of bringing glory to God alone. So now when I get stuck, that is where I go. My prayers are songs of worship glorifying my God and King. God is bigger than "The Beast" and He is working in it and through it in ways we may never see.

Oh, the depth of the riches of the wisdom and knowledge of God!

How unsearchable his judgments,

and his paths beyond tracing out!

"Who has known the mind of the Lord?

Or who has been his counselor?"

"Who has ever given to God,

that God should repay them?"

For from him and through him and for him are all things.

To him be the glory forever! Amen.

Romans 11:33-36 NIV

Diane (active living devotee)

There are moments in our lives that define and shape us. May 3rd was such a moment in my life. That day will be forever etched into my entire being. Not just because of the stress of being in the middle of the largest evacuation in Canadian history, but because that was the day my son became my hero. And the day I stopped looking for God in the shadows but saw Him in Technicolor.

There were many acts of kindness and people that supported us on the journey - from stores that gave us discounts that made us weep, to churches that opened their doors to us, to my husband's employer that opened up housing for many families and the piano store that gave me unrestricted access to their finest grand piano so I could prepare for my music exam.

We felt God working in so many ways. He has not provided for all our wants (we want to go home but can't as our home is in a restricted area due to the damage) but He has more than provided for our needs.

Some people may think God should have stopped the fire. He could have, but He didn't. That would have been too easy. I think He wanted people to look for Him in other ways.

Elizabeth (artist)

My supervisor texted me and asked when I would be back to Fort McMurray. I told her in the middle of June. She found me a family who needed many hours and also two other families came back to Fort McMurray. Then a few weeks later, I was given another client. God is faithful! He replaced all the hours I lost plus more. He continues to provide for me.

I am also content to be where God wants me to be. I am more concerned about people and spiritual things, even more than I used to be, since the fire. People are important.

After being back in Fort McMurray, I had to stay at my sister's place until I had my apartment cleaned. That following long weekend, I was invited to go to a summer family camp.

My friend and I spoke to a man who had relatives in Fort McMurray. He said that something unusual happened to him; something out of the ordinary we would not be accustomed to hearing about. The Lord showed him a scene as if a war was happening: fire, explosions, and people fleeing. God told him to pray for everyone to get out. He thought that it was in the Middle East.

He went to a prayer meeting and told everyone about what God had showed him, and they prayed for everyone to get out safely. I shared with him about two dreams I had.

My dreams showed stars on a map of North America. I later found out that the stars on the maps represent people. They are spoken of in Daniel 12:3 (MSG):

Men and women who have lived wisely and well will shine brilliantly, like the cloudless, star-strewn night skies. And those who put others on the right path to life will glow like stars forever.

It amazed me to see how much God cares and would even speak to a man to pray for people he doesn't even know. But God knows everyone by name. It is not God's will that anyone should perish, but that all should come to saving knowledge of Him.

Danelle (work-at-home mom)

August 30th

We have just received word that we are allowed to return to our home tomorrow.

Thank you, Jesus, for keeping us safe.

Thank you for pushing me to leave when we did.

Thank you for getting us over that berm and through the ditch.

Thank you for the police officers and others who were directing traffic to get us out.

Thank you for the full tank of gas and keeping us safe while we drove to Edmonton.

Thank you for amazing friends who opened their home to us without hesitation.

Thank you for getting Drew back to us safely.

Thank you for all the generous donations and gifts which made those weeks away from home more tolerable.

Thank you for all the first responders who worked endlessly to save everything they could.

Thank you for a place to live together as a family in Fort McMurray until our house is ready to go back to.

Thank you for a loving and supportive church family.

And...

Thank you for the rain.

Trish (storyteller)

It is nothing short of miraculous.

It hit me that there are so many people who were "just doing their jobs" through all of this, but because they did their jobs, we got out safely, our city was protected, and we have something to come back to. I am beyond words, beyond all feelings of gratitude. So good to be home.

David (firefighter with three sons)

January 2016

Through that process, God replaced the camper that burned; God replaced the truck that burned because it was (insured) with the house; we got a house that was nicer than the one we had before, which was incredible. As of October, we moved in; now it's January and we're completely settled.

We had our third boy, Jackson, at the end of August and that was a blessing, too. He had an umbilical verix, which was a condition which essentially is a bubble on the umbilical cord and causes a turbulent flow of blood and can damage the cells. There are a whole bunch of (potential) problems with that; if it ruptures it can be fatal.

Jen had to be induced a month early so we were down in Edmonton for that. We shipped the kids off to Vancouver; my sister was awesome—she took the kids for a couple of weeks while we went to Edmonton and this all sorted out and we had our third child.

As soon as he was born, the umbilical verix became a moot point, and it was a true blessing. That's why we called him Jackson. It means God is gracious. We thought it was fitting, considering all we'd been through with losing the house, and the complications with the pregnancy. We mulled over a whole bunch of names and that one seemed appropriate.

We're settled in. Now we're in a position where we can start helping people. Some didn't even lose their homes but had a lot of damage and haven't been able to get their insurance to help them renovate. We are praying for them.

It's been interesting seeing the other side of things. It'll probably look like this for two or three years, until we can see everybody settled.

We were blessed that we were back in place in seven months. It's pretty incredible.

I didn't feel like we were super tested or anything. But I think I was fairly materialistic. My focus was too much on the things of the world. When we lost everything, I thought things would be more devastating than they were. It was a good way to refocus. All these things can come, they can go; they aren't really ours. They are on loan from the Lord. If he wants to take it all away, he can.

If we have our family and our health, we're okay.

We're at a place where we don't have any needs and we can be a blessing to others.

Michael (layperson)

I hadn't tried hounding (my previous company for a job). I knew the Lord was in charge. I'd received an email. I knew I had to use the time to work on the book. So I did that and waited.

Early July, my friend Dave gave me a shout and told me he was working again and asked if I wanted to go for dinner on him. Very thankful for the offer, I asked where he wanted to go.

He said "I don't care where we go, you pick."

I felt like a burger but wanted to go somewhere with a variety so he'd be happy. After all, I was so grateful to get a free meal which meant one more day without needing to go back to work. So I offered, "Boston Pizza."

"No way," he responded in his typical gruff manner. "I don't want to eat there."

"Okay, well I feel like a burger, so... Fatburger is good. Or Original Joes?"

"Yeah, okay, Original Joes it is!"

So Dave comes and we're on our way there in my car when suddenly he reaches down and holds his belly, "I feel like rice..."

I was grateful for the coming meal, so I acquiesced to my brother.

He continues, "How about that place over by the college... in that mini-mall..." "You mean Wok Box?" I ask.

"Yeah, Wok Box."

"Sure, man, Wok Box is good," I said.

We drive there and walk inside. There's an eating area to the right and the whole establishment is partitioned by a row of booths from the entrance up the middle and towards the front counter where you order. You can see over the booths which are very high, and view people waiting for their order towards the drink refrigerators.

At the end of the booths is a large square column that rises up towards the ceiling. There's a guy leaning against it. All I can see are his shoulders covered by a light blue, dark blue lined plaid shirt, and the back of his brown hair, but I have a strange feeling inside.

I thought, 'That is my general manager from (the company where I worked) who I've only met once. He's the one sending us all those communication emails to let people know what was developing.'

Then Dave says to him, "Hey, Clayton!" and goes to talk.

Sure enough, I was right. Don't know how, but I was right. Maybe it was God? I figure, I'll talk to him after I order. So I place my order while Dave talks, then I move over to await the order being filled and nonchalantly greet Clayton with a smile and a handshake.

"Hi, Clayton. I just want to say thanks so much for keeping everyone in the loop every day. I know that probably helped bring a lot of peace and reassurance to people at a difficult time."

He replies as if it was nothing, "Oh of course man, I feel it's my responsibility to take care of you guys." Then his expression changes slightly, bemusedly he says, "Sorry I don't recognize you, are you new?"

I smile, "Yeah, I got hired four days before the fire."

His eyes brighten and cheerfully he says, "Oh okay! Well how's everything going now? Back to work yet?"

Lightly I say, "Nope, not yet."

Concerned, Clayton replies, "Oh, is everything going alright money wise?"

I feign mild despair and sigh while stroking five days of facial hair I've been growing.

"Well, it's gotten so tough I've had to save on razors."

Shocked, Clayton says, "REALLY?!"

I chuckle, "No, no, just kidding, I don't shave often if I don't have to, things are fine."

Clayton laughs too, and I add, "I got the e-sign letter so I'm just waiting on the call to return."

Now he's a little puzzled, "Well, that doesn't sound right. If you got the rehire letter, you'd be told when to return to work also."

I raise my brows uncertain of what to make of that.

He continues, "What's your name again? I'll email HR tomorrow and have Gabrielle line you up."

Pleased, I say, "Oh okay, it's Michael Hill." And that's that.

Clayton takes his order to go and Dave and I enjoy ours there and start to talk about what just transpired. I get a call the next day, and orientation a day later and I'm back to work.

I am not surprised by the providence of God but still a little in awe. Why was a district manager at Wok Box when he could've eaten somewhere better? Why did Dave call me for a free bite to eat? Why did he suddenly get the craving for rice? Why was I submissive in where we went? Because God is God.

I had no intention of calling them for work. It turns out the e-sign email I'd gotten was just something about working on a site after the fire or whatever and had nothing to do with my rehire.

However, there I was back to work. And no coincidence, I ended up on Dave's team, not even knowing Dave was working for the same company as me! And just in time as the bank notified me it would be withdrawing money for the mortgage again come September.

Praise God, Hallelujah. He is Jehovah Jireh, my provider!

Cyndy (composer)

We returned home on the 2nd of June. Our home was undamaged, untouched. We cleaned out our fridge and that was all that we needed to do. Al had had the presence of mind to turn off the fan on the furnace before we left on that May evening. There was not even a hint of smoke smell in our house.

I know that many people lost their homes or suffered varying degrees of damage. My heart aches for them. But that was not at all our experience.

I have thought a lot about my response when people ask how the fire affected us. My first response was, that we were very blessed. This is true and yet does that mean that people who lost their homes were not? I don't believe that at all.

If I had lost my possessions I would still have to say that I was blessed. The thing most important to me - my family - was safe. So I am blessed.

What if I had lost someone in the fire? I would still have to say I am blessed. That is a lesson I learned when the Lord took our 14 month old grandson Milo home to heaven in 2011. I am still blessed. This world with all its good and its bad is truly not my home. I am just passing through. God has given me much. I feel blessed beyond measure. But if it is all taken away, I still have Him.

My second response was that I'm thankful to God. Once again I had to re-evaluate. If I had lost my home, would that mean I would not be thankful? No. I am learning to be thankful in all circumstances.

We moved away from Fort McMurray in October. I loved Fort Mac and had no desire to leave. But Al needed to get off the two and a half hour daily bus ride schedule. He now flies in to work Monday mornings and comes home Thursday nights.

Most of our children remained in Fort McMurray. But the Lord has sustained me and even brought sweetness into a time that I thought would be quite negative. And I am learning over and over again that I brought nothing into this world and it is certain I can carry nothing out of it. So as long as I have food and clothing I will be content.

I suppose this may be a lesson I will be learning as long as I live. I expect it is a lesson particularly difficult in a first world country. There are always things clawing at us.

But when you lose (or think you've lost) all your things, you realize they aren't that important after all. God is with us - Emmanuel. That is the message we hear over and over at Christmas.

It is just as true on May 3rd as it is on December 25. God is with us. And if He is with me, I have everything that I need. And if such a time comes, when I don't have the physical things that I truly need, I will go home to be with Jesus. And I will have everything. And I will be blessed.

Jonathan (firefighter novelist)

There were many sights, sounds and experiences that I will never forget. That week fighting fires mirrored my time at war in Afghanistan. During that fire, Fort McMurray was a war zone, and each of us fought on many of its battlefields. But the difference here is that we were fighting against a force of nature for our very homes.

As all wars do, this eventually came to an end. Let me tell you, the feeling of being reunited with my wife and unborn child after having accepted the idea that I may never see them again was a feeling I cannot even begin to describe other than calling it pure joy. Two weeks later, we welcomed a baby boy into the world. We named him Asher, which appropriately means 'happy' and 'blessed.'

As a firefighter, I worked as tirelessly as I felt I could with my brothers and sisters and those that had come to our aid to hold back the fire and save as many homes as we could.

As a Christian, I prayed through it all that we would succeed, that those that were hurting would be comforted, and for the health and safety of all of us fighting.

To me, that was the most miraculous aspect of the entire fire. Despite all of the chaos; the collapsing houses, the fire-ravaged streets and forests, steady stream of explosions, and the intense heat and smoke, not one of us first responders lost their life, or was seriously injured. All of us knew our job and did the best we could with what we had to fight the fight that had been thrown upon us.

Through it all, it would have been easy to doubt. To ask why. To wish it didn't have to happen. I think that is where my faith helped me react differently.

Through it all, I never doubted God. Instead He gave me the fortitude to acknowledge His hand. I thanked Him for giving me the life and trials I had gone through before, that had prepared me for this fight. I thank Him for all the good that comes out of a fight like this: more hope, more character, more service, more love.

Joe (RCMP & Harley rider)

Now, I have to say, I don't feel like a hero, nor like the hero my friends were thanking me for being. I'm a police officer, and maybe I don't see it the same way. I see the call for duty, no matter how tragic, is simply what we do.

In our world, dealing with tragedy or situations when things or people are at their worst, is something that becomes normal to us. We, on a routine basis, deal with situations that are abnormal in most people's lives. Again, it's what we do.

I remember when I was little, my mom worked at the hospital and knew all the police officers. I remember being with her one time and being so mesmerized by an officer's duty belt and the gun, wondering what it was like to carry a gun on your hip all day. After 21 years of wearing a duty belt, it becomes no different than putting your watch on in the morning.

I recall Shaquille O'Neill posted a video on Facebook of himself sending a "Thank you to the incredible first responders in Fort McMurray. You guys are the true heroes." Now I don't respond to a lot of things I see on social media, but this one hit a bit of a note with me and I felt compelled to respond to his video. I don't know if he ever read it, but I think it grasps something about who the real heroes were during the wildfire:

"Mr. Shaq, my wife and I have been in Fort McMurray since last Tuesday (with a short break). We are both police officers and two of our kids live there and I have a cousin there. Thank you for saluting the first responders, which covers a wide variety of professions. Although the many people who have come to Fort McMurray as a call of duty, and although that does seem to be heroic, I have to say this... The true heroes are those fire fighters, ambulance, police, essential city employees and those employed throughout the community who had to part ways with their families as they fled the community while they remained behind to save their community. They Sir, are the real heroes. They dug in and worked countless hours in the early days while some of them knew they lost everything, their homes and their priceless treasures that can never be replaced. The fact that one firefighter fought to save a home of a family whose daughter died in a collision while traveling to safety; to save the memories for the family while his own home burned to the ground a block away .These people Sir, they are the real heroes of the devastation that will last a lifetime in the memories of many of us who answered the call for duty."

Police officers and emergency services personnel around the world are always affected by the things we see each day. Again, dealing with tragic events, people at their worst, and the most abnormal situations, are commonplace to the profession. When you see us we may seem to be unaffected, to some heartless, but we bleed when we are cut, and we cry when we hurt; it's just that in your circumstance we have to stand tall to deal with the situation.

Never think for a moment that we don't feel the pain of a victim or have nothing in our own experiences to relate to what is happening at that point. There are often times when I reflect on my career and remember those I have helped; recalling events and situations as though they happened yesterday. And I know, that I was forever changed by them.

EPILOGUE

Dee (poet)

Some environmentalists said the wildfire was the result of global warming. Someone said it was bad karma for producing dirty oil. Many said it was caused by human activity, an ATV rider flicking a cigarette into dry brush. The majority said it was a normal forest fire cycle, necessary to bring new life. Insurance companies said the fire was an Act of God.

There were preachers who prayed Fort McMurrayites would repent of their selfish lifestyles; others rushed to her aid, remembering the generosity of the city when crisis struck elsewhere.

Regardless of Fort McMurray's image problems at times, many people will continue to come in search of a better life. They will see the places of worship, the fire halls, the police stations, hospital, and rebuilt neighbourhoods.

They comforted and consoled (Job) over all the trouble the Lord had brought on him, and each one gave him a piece of silver and a gold ring. The Lord blessed the latter part of Job's life more than the former part.

Job 42:11b-12a, NIV

All my worries came to nothing. The oil sands plants started up without a hitch. They are extracting the blackest, richest material they have ever seen.

As we rolled out of town towing a trailer of assorted furniture and boxes, we drove through our neighbourhood where we'd taken countless walks with our dogs on the trails; through Downtown where my husband and I had lived in our first apartment together and bought a house among mature trees where we'd lived for 20 years; and the high school where I'd gone and the college where I'd graduated, and the hospital where all my babies had been born.

And I saw the steeple of the church I'd seen from a field when I was a teen, out way past late, wondering if there really was a God. And at the same steeple we spent many Christmas Eve services together, singing carols, welcoming in the Christ.

Next we drove near the high school where Judi had lived; the girl who'd first told me that Jesus wanted to have a relationship with me. Past Abasand where I'd first moved-in with my dad and skipped school to hang out with friends, where Jeff and I had bought our first house and we'd ridden our ATV on dusty trails down to the Horse River with our yellow Lab, Pux.

Past Waterways we kept on, where we'd fished on the Clearwater River and swam in the shallows on hot summer days; past Beacon Hill where I'd visited friends for tea, baby showers, and birthday parties.

We drove past Gregoire where we'd washed our vehicles and had our wedding reception in the Sawridge, and where the coworker had lived who pulled a Bible out at break time in an oil sands mine and reminded me that Jesus loved me, and did I want to know Him better? I did and over the years, I grew to love God there in Fort McMurray.

Then we drove past the Discovery Centre where I'd worked at Tourism and kids played on the front end of a heavy hauler, smaller than the ones at the mine which I'd driven. And we passed Airport Road and to Saprae Creek and our friends on acreages where we'd visited for fun days.

And beyond that, Vista Ridge, where me and all our children had learned to ski and we spent many family days. Then we passed Gregoire Lake where we'd camped and fished, spent summer afternoons playing in the sand.

Later, we passed Stoney Mountain where I remembered playing Vivaldi's Ring of Mystery for our kids as we headed to swim at Maqua Lake and pick wild strawberries.

We gave Gravol to O'Malley this time and he didn't throw up until Red Deer. Stubbs travelled fine, though his scales felt cool to the touch. Cay also came to live her senior years with us in Southern Alberta, to try and catch elusive gophers and nap on the sunny deck, the wind playing in her fur.

There is a river close by and sometimes we take Cay and O'Malley for walks and they romp in the water. O'Malley barks at the invisible monster that lives in the rapids. In the summer, we will swim in it and ride floaties over the rocks. And over time we will learn where the good fishing spots are, and where to pick berries.

I am amazed to see where we landed, far from our home in Fort McMurray in just a few short months. We sometimes feel anxious, but we are slowly healing.

After Christmas, my husband was ready to use our new firepit with our younger son. And we are choosing which trees to plant, but they won't be close to our house.

Many others in Fort McMurray have much more to deal with: wrestling with their insurance companies, damage to their standing homes, uncertainty, stress, sudden change, severe PTSD, survivor's guilt. When I think of my friends and old neighbours rebuilding and struggling, my heart melts. I ask God to heal them and to bless them; I ask God to strengthen them, and return to them more than they have lost.

Statistics

The wildfire began on May 1, 2016.

About 90,000 people fled Fort McMurray and area, the largest evacuation in Alberta history. Two young people died as they fled. (The Globe and Mail and Global News)

State of Emergency declared on May 4, which lasted two months. Military were called in to help. Airlifts took place, and other aircraft were held on standby at Cold Lake. (CTV News)

2,400 structures were destroyed; many more sustained extensive smoke-damage. 19 oil sites were endangered. One lodge with 665 units was destroyed. 590,000 hectares (1,500,000 acres) of forest was consumed by the wildfire. (Government of Alberta and Wikipedia)

1,572 firefighters and support staff; 60 helicopters, 19 tankers, and 37 pieces of heavy equipment were used to fight fires in Alberta, in June 2016. Crews completed more than 535 km of dozer firebreaks. (Alberta Forestry)

It was the costliest Canadian disaster ever recorded, at $3.58 billion (CAD) insured losses. Uninsured and under-insured losses are undetermined. (CBC News)

It was confirmed under control on July 5, 2016. (Wikipedia)

Editor's Note

Editing this book was much more difficult than I had ever expected. After working for an hour or more, I would look up and have to drag myself into the present and realize I am not in my evacuation lodgings. Still my overriding thought is, "How gracious is God". We saw his hand in countless ways. We experienced his love and provision both through human agency and through direct divine intervention.

As I read the accounts of others, it brought to mind incidents I had forgotten and connected the dots I had missed. "Into every life a little rain must fall." An old adage perhaps, but there is truth in it. The question is, what affect will that rain have on the soul? It can flood and destroy, or it can cause us to grow and flourish. It is my hope that the testimony of these Fort McMurray survivors will help others to recognize the God who is present, willing and able to meet us at our point of need. He is able to save to the uttermost.

~Cyndy Pickersgill

Photos on Back Cover

[Clockwise from top.]

Firefighter David Oger. Submitted photo.

Trish Collins with Cokie. Selfie taken August 2015.

Christine MacKay with firefighter husband Chris, and sons, five-year-old Chase, and three-year-old Finlay. Christine is pregnant in the photo (taken August 2016), with baby Levi, born September 16, 2016.

Wina Reid and daughter Kelsey, Mothers' Day, Edmonton, May 2016.

Firefighter Jonathan Gillies with his wife Amanda, Edmonton, May 2016.

Centre: burned Harley Davidson collector motorcycle, Waterways, Fort McMurray, May 2016. Submitted photo.

Discover the website MuscleAndHeart at **http://www.deebentley.com**

Like the Facebook Page **Muscle And Heart–Fort McMurray Fire Stories**

Interact on **Twitter #ymmFireStories**

Write a book review on **Amazon .com** or **Amazon.ca**

Special Thanks

To Michael Hill, for encouragement and help wrangling submissions.

To Cyndy Pickersgill, for extensive editing and humour which kept me going.

To Bill Bunn, YA author and mentor to many, for valuable feedback.

To my husband Jeff, for limitless love, patience, support; and for being my chef. You may cook for me any day, Hon.

~Dee Bentley

Made in the USA
Charleston, SC
27 February 2017